Robin —
With love from
the Pinkhams.

LEITH'S GUIDE TO WINE

Prue Leith and Richard Harvey

BLOOMSBURY

First published in Great Britain 1995

Bloomsbury Publishing Plc, 2 Soho Square, London W1V 5DE

Copyright © 1995 by Leith's School of Food and Wine Ltd

The moral right of the authors has been asserted

A CIP catalogue record for this book is available from the British Library

ISBN 0 7475 1827 0

10 9 8 7 6 5 4 3 2 1

Typeset by Hewer Text Composition Services, Edinburgh
Printed by WBC Ltd, Bridgend, South Wales

Illustrations by Bill Sanderson
Maps by Neil Hyslop
Designed by Carroll Associates

CONTENTS

FOREWORD

Most people will tell you that the reason you need to know about wine is so you don't feel outfaced by wine waiters in restaurants, so you know what to look for in supermarkets, or so you can lay down a modest cellar today and sell it for a fortune later.

But for me, knowing a little about wine (and I don't know a lot – Richard is this book's expert author) has been the source of enormous pleasure over the years. An interest in wine is the link that binds the most unlikely people together. I've made instant, if transient, friends with fellow travellers on South African Airways, on New Zealand sheep-farms, on salmon rivers in Iceland, in Hong Kong hotels and on British Rail, all because of a common interest in the grape.

And the interests lasts forever. The wine trade, especially in the last ten years, has developed enormously, with New World wines sometimes teaching the great classic wine countries of Europe a trick or two, and striving always to match, if not outdo, the great masters. And wine writing, especially in England, is extraordinarily good, and it's hard to limit one's reading to the food and wine pages of the papers – you end up, like fly-fishing enthusiasts or motorcar buffs, buying a raft of specialist wine magazines, and dreaming of wines you'll never be able to afford, or sending off for little-known ones that you can.

When I opened Leith's Restaurant in 1969 I thought I was a hot-stuff cook, and it never occurred to me that I ought also to know something about wine. A friend introduced me to Cyril Ray, one of the most amusing and down-to-earth of wine writers, and he put together my first wine list for me. I still have a copy. It wasn't long, but it did include 1955 Lafite, and 1961 La Tache. No wonder I got the wine bug.

I first met Richard Harvey, the real brains and tastebuds behind this book when, as a nineteen-year-old drop-out from Architecture, he came to work at my party catering business as a casual delivery-man. He soon swapped to a barman's uniform and began to serve the drinks – and the wines. Within a year, he'd found his life-long passion, and had left us to join the wine trade.

Today Richard spends his time seeking out wonderful wines for his customers, or turning the students at Leith's School of Food and Wine, if not always into absolute *aficionados*, at least into confident, knowledgeable enthusiasts. No one who goes on a 'study-trip' to France with Richard will ever forget it, or him.

This book is like him: practical, helpful, informative, but, I hope, never stodgy.

Prue Leith

CHAPTER ONE

WHERE WINE
IS MADE

———

In order to grow grapes for wine production, the vine needs the right climate and the right soil. It is the combination of the vine variety, grown on a particular soil, in a specific climate, with the vagaries of each individual year and the producer's practices in the vineyard and in the cellar that will create the style of a wine.

CLIMATE

The ideal conditions for the vine are a temperate climate, with sufficiently warm summers to ripen the grapes, but cool winters to allow the vine to rest. The majority of the world's vineyards are found between the latitudes of 30–50° north and south of the equator, where the annual mean temperature is between 10 and 20°C. Wines can be produced outside these limits – the United Kingdom, for instance, has vineyards at 51° latitude – but vine-growing here is very marginal. Similarly, not every area within these bands is wholly suitable for grape-growing.

It has been calculated by the University of Southern California at Davis that the minimum heat-summation for growing grapes for wine, measured in degree-days, is 1000 degree days, Centigrade. A figure is arrived at by multiplying the average daily temperature above 10°C by the number of days in the growing season. The Mosel Valley in Germany is in fact just below 1000 degree days, whereas Sonoma County, California, achieves twice that figure. The vine would ideally like 1500 hours of sunshine during the growing season and 100 mm of rain, mostly in the winter and spring.

There will obviously be large differences between wines grown at the cooler and hotter latitudes. Wines from cool climates will usually have higher levels of acidity and lower degrees of grape sugar, which will mean less alcohol and less body. Cooler areas are better suited to the production of white wines, which require a degree of acidity to give them bite. Black grapes generally need longer to ripen, and therefore the warmer zones are more suited to the production of red wines. Whether red or white, wines from hotter climates will tend to be fuller, richer and more alcoholic as a result of being made from riper grapes.

Microclimates

There are several factors which can alter the general climate in specific areas, and therefore determine whether wine can be produced and its particular style.

Aspect

The exposure of a vineyard will have an important bearing on the wine produced. In cool areas it is important that the vineyards face south or south-east to gain maximum benefit from the sun, whereas in hotter zones, vineyards may be better placed facing west or even north to prevent excessive exposure. Vineyards in cool climates are better sited on slopes to gain more direct sunlight.

Altitude

Altitude has an important effect on the average mean temperature; every 100 m above sea-level, the temperature drops 1°C. Many vineyards in Chile lie north of 30° south, but are planted at high altitude, where the temperature is much lower. Similarly, mountain ranges can protect vineyards from wind and rain; the vineyards of Alsace in north-eastern France lie on the eastern slopes of the Vosges mountains, and enjoy a much drier climate than that part of Germany which lies across the river Rhine. Slopes also give good drainage; many vineyards are planted in the middle of a slope. The tops are usually too exposed, the valley floors too prone to frost pockets, as well as having a richer soil.

Water

Proximity to the coast will usually moderate the climate, for example around Bordeaux in south-west France and the Napa Valley in California, whereas the continental situation of Germany's vineyards helps to maintain temperature in what is otherwise a marginal area. Rivers will have a different effect – the movement of water will help reduce the effect of frosts, particularly important in the Mosel Valley in Germany. They will also raise the ambient temperature by reflection. Rivers can help create the humidity which is necessary for the development of botrytis, or 'noble rot', which is essential to the production of fine sweet wines. Irrigation is practised in many of the hotter wine-producing areas, particularly Australia, although within the EC it is not allowed during the summer months for quality wines produced from specified regions.

SOIL

Many vineyards are planted on soils which are too poor to support any other crop. A vine will produce better-quality grapes if it has to strive for nourishment than if it is planted in a rich, fertile soil. The vine needs a well-drained soil to encourage a deep root structure. In wet and fertile areas, the roots will stay near the surface and the vine will tend to be too vigorous and crop too heavily. In well-drained soils the roots will have to travel deeper into the subsoil to find water and will be more likely to find the nutrients and minerals which will feed the grapes and later flavour the wine.

Most of the classic wine-producing regions of Europe have been established on a geographical basis, which took account of the soil in each particular area. Outside Europe, vineyards have been planted where the climate is suitable, without recourse to soil type. In France, where the concept of *terroir* is enshrined in legislation, it would be argued that the limestone in Champagne and Sancerre encourages the production of wines with acidity, whilst the granite of the Beaujolais hills helps reduce the acidity of the Gamay grape.

Alternatively, many producers in the New World would argue that the soil, as long as it is well drained, has very little influence on the composition of the wine.

However, where the soil definitely does affect the vine is in those areas where heat reflection increases the temperature. The slate of the Mosel Valley in Germany, and the round pudding stones of the southern Rhone Valley in France have an important bearing on the style of the wine of these regions.

GRAPE VARIETY

Practically all the wines of the world come from one species of vine, *Vitis vinifera*. However, nearly all *Vitis vinifera* are grafted on to rootstock of other species as a result of phylloxera. *Phylloxera vastratix* is an aphid bug which arrived in Europe from America in 1860, and proceeded to devastate the vineyards by attacking the roots of the vines. Many remedies were tried, such as fumigating and flooding the soil, but the only satisfactory recourse was to species of American vines, which are resistant to the aphid.

Unfortunately the wine produced from American vines had a distinctly 'foxy' character. So today nearly all vineyards are planted with *vinifera* vines grafted onto American rootstock. Throughout the vine-growing world there are pockets that are still planted with ungrafted vines, but it is really only Chile that has completely escaped the presence of phylloxera.

The selection of rootstock is made from *Vitis berlandieri*, *riparia* or *rupestris* or, more usually, from a crossing of these

American vines. The rootstock must be compatible not only with the *vinifera* variety, but also with the soil and the climate in which it will be grown. Most grafting is done by nurseries, who provide vineyard owners with virus-free stock ready-grafted for planting straight out in the vineyard.

Hybrid vines, that is, a crossing between *vinifera* and American vines, have been produced, although only one, Seyval Blanc, has been remotely successful. No quality wine produced from a specified region within the EC may be made from hybrid vines.

The choice of grape variety is not always an option open to the vineyard owner. Within the EC, particularly for specified quality wines, the permitted grape varieties are clearly stipulated. For instance, Chablis can only be produced from Chardonnay, and Beaujolais from Gamay, whilst red Bordeaux and Chianti are allowed up to 5 varieties. These are usually varieties which have traditionally been grown in the area, although Chianti is unusual in that Cabernet-Sauvignon is a non-native variety which is now permitted in the blend after much pressure from producers. In the New World, which does not have the same restrictions applied to appellations, growers are free to plant the varieties they feel will best suit their climate and soil. A vineyard owner in Coonawarra, Australia can plant Cabernet-Sauvignon, Riesling and Chardonnay beside each other. A grower in Bordeaux can plant Cabernet-Sauvignon, but is not allowed to plant Riesling or Chardonnay.

The major varieties of *Vitis vinifera* are as follows:

Red

Cabernet-Sauvignon is considered the classic variety of Bordeaux, where it is almost always blended with at least two other varieties, and, with the exception of the Médoc and Graves, usually comprises less than 50 per cent of the blend. It is also grown successfully, and often unblended, in many other vineyard areas, notably California, Australia, South Africa, South America, Italy and Bulgaria. It produces well-coloured wines with distinctive blackcurrant fruit flavours, good tannins and acidity.

Pinot Noir is the classic variety of Burgundy, but unlike Cabernet-Sauvignon has not been successful elsewhere, although it constitutes a large part of Champagne. It likes a cool climate and produces generally light-coloured wines with soft, vegetal fruit flavours.

Syrah is the classic variety of the northern Rhône, but it is also grown extensively in the south of France, and in Australia, where it is known as the Shiraz. It produces deep-coloured wines, with plenty of tannin and a spicy, mineral flavour.

Merlot is the most widely planted variety in Bordeaux. It is usually blended with Cabernet-Sauvignon, although the most expensive red wine of the region, Château Pétrus, is almost wholly Merlot. It produces soft, plummy wines with high alcohol and low acidity, which mature relatively quickly.

Gamay is the sole variety of Beaujolais, where it produces light, fruity wines, high in acidity, for early drinking.

Nebbiolo is the grape of Piedmont in north-west Italy, producing Barolo and Barbaresco. It makes powerful wines, high in tannin and acidity with a tarry, liquorice bouquet.

Zinfandel, almost exclusively grown in California (some is also being produced in South Africa), produces a fruity, blackberry-ish red wine, the best being quite intense and complex. It is also used to make white wine and especially rosé, or 'blush' wine.

White

Chardonnay, the classic variety of Burgundy, is also successfully grown throughout the world, especially Australia, New Zealand and California, and also in Champagne. When the wine is made from low yields, it has a rich, buttery concentration, with alcohol and body. It is one of the few white varieties that can support fermentation and ageing in wood.

Riesling, which produces the best wines of Germany, is also grown in Alsace, Austria, California, Australia and New Zealand. It is sometimes described as Rheinriesling, or Rhine Riesling or Johannisberg Riesling to distinguish it from Welschriesling, a lesser varietal. It can produce steely, dry wine, as in Alsace, and a medium to sweeter fruitier style, but with high acidity, as in Germany. New World Rieslings have less acidity and more body.

Sauvignon is the grape of Pouilly-Fumé and Sancerre in the Loire, but is also grown in Bordeaux, New Zealand, Australia and California (where it is often referred to as Fumé Blanc, which originally meant that it was matured in oak, although today the terms Sauvignon Blanc and Fumé Blanc are interchangeable). It can have a pungent aroma of gooseberries, and be aggressively fruity with high acidity, particularly in the cool zones of the Loire and New Zealand; when grown in warmer climates, it has more weight and less pungency.

Muscat is grown throughout the world. It has a distinctive, perfumed, grapey aroma. Although it can be made dry – the best come from Alsace – it is more often made into a sweet wine, particularly in Australia and California. It is often fortified, as in the south of France and Portugal, and made sparkling in Italy as for Asti Spumante.

Semillon is the variety responsible for the classic sweet wines of Bordeaux. Its thin skin makes it susceptible to the botrytis necessary for the production of sweet wines, but it can also make dry wines, again in Bordeaux, and in Australia, which are quite fat, with low acidity and a waxy flavour.

Chenin Blanc is principally grown in the Loire, where it is known as the Pineau de la Loire, and produces wines with high acidity and appley flavour, which can be dry, medium or sweet, still or sparkling. The best sweet wines age well. It is also grown in South Africa, where it is known as the Steen, and makes fresh, medium-dry wines, often with a slight sparkle.

11

Gewürztraminer is the most characteristic grape of Alsace but is also grown in Germany, Austria, California and New Zealand. It has a distinctive aroma, reminiscent of dried rose-petals, and a fat, rich flavour of lychees; it is usually dry but can be sweet if late-harvested.

Crosses

There are several crossing of *Vitis vinifera*. These are not to be confused with hybrids, but are crossings of two species. The best known is Müller-Thurgau, a Riesling/Sylvaner cross, which is the most widely planted variety in Germany, producing wines with soft, grapey aromas and little acidity.

VITICULTURE

Planting

There are different views on density of planting, but this will often depend on the method of pruning and training to be adopted. Many vineyards are now harvested by machine rather than by hand, which will determine the plan of planting. Most vines are planted out ready-grafted, and it will be 3 years before they will bear any fruit, although this production is often not allowed to be used for a quality wine. It is usually from the fourth year that the vine will crop successfully, but it will not really be fully established until the tenth year. From 10 to 25 years the vine will usually crop at its optimum; after 25 years the yields will diminish, although the quality will improve. The grower will have to decide at what time it is economic to uproot the vines and replant the vineyard; normally this is around 40 to 50 years of age, although some growers will keep a plot of very old vines, perhaps to make a special blend.

Pruning

The vine has to be pruned every year to allow sufficient buds to produce the fruit, and to prepare the wood from which the buds will produce in the following year. The number of buds left on the vine in the spring will determine the amount of fruit produced at harvest. By reducing the number of buds, the grower will restrict the yield, and produce a more concentrated wine. Under the controls for quality wines in France and Italy the permitted yields are incorporated in the Appellation Contrôlée and Denominazione de Origine regulations for each area. However, any serious-minded producer will seek to maximize the potential for his wine by selective pruning.

Pruning will also be carried out during the growing season to restrict the vegetation, so as to concentrate the growth of the vine into the fruit, and to regulate the leaf canopy to give the fruit either greater or lesser exposure to the sun.

Training

More and more vineyards now have vines trained on wires spaced wide enough to allow for mechanical harvesting. However, many of the vineyards of southern France and Spain still allow the vines to grow in low bushes. In both cases the pruning leaves a number of short spurs with 2 or 3 buds which will grow into the fruiting canes of that year. The more traditional cane pruning of Bordeaux and Burgundy, known as Guyot, replaces the wood every year with one or two new canes trained along wires.

The vine can suffer from the weather and various pests and diseases during the course of the year.

Weather

Spring frost is the greatest danger to vines because it will kill the delicate young buds. The traditional remedy was to burn fires in the vineyards, but now many areas that are particularly prone have installed aspersion systems. These spray water on to the vines, when there is a threat of frost, which forms a protective coating of ice around the bud.

Cold, rainy weather at pollination can affect the flowering and prevent the fruit from setting. These two problems are known as *coulure* and *millerandage*. Rain at harvest-time can severely dilute the wine and cause problems with rotten fruit which will taint the wine.

Hail can be very destructive once the grapes have set on the vine, as it will break the skins and cause the fruit to rot.

In Burgundy, rockets are sometimes fired into the clouds, or planes sent up to seed the clouds and cause rain, rather than hail, to fall.

Disease

Throughout the growing season the vines will be sprayed to protect them against a variety of fungal diseases. Traditional spraying was with Bordeaux mixture, containing copper sulphate and lime, and sulphur, which were effective against mildew and rot. The bluish tinge on the leaves of vines during the summer indicates that they had been sprayed with copper sulphate. Today, systemic sprays which quickly enter the plant's capillary system are often used and these are more effective, especially in areas with high rainfall, which can otherwise wash away the effects of traditional sprays.

Pests

These are mostly combated by insecticide sprays, with the exception of *Phylloxera vastatrix*, mentioned on page 7. Obviously wines which are sold as organic will not be treated with such sprays.

Soil

Mineral deficiencies in the soil can be corrected with fertilizers. Again, organic wines will require that only natural fertilizers have been used in the vineyard.

Harvest

The harvest usually takes place in September and October in the northern hemisphere and February and March in the southern hemisphere. The time of picking will be determined by the sugar content of the grape, which will give an indication of the potential degree of alcohol of the resulting wine. The acids in the grape will diminish as the sugar content increases. White varieties are normally harvested first, as white wine requires a higher degree of acidity.

Harvesting is still carried out by hand, particularly for sweet white wines. Red wine vineyards, especially those planted on flat land, are increasingly being harvested mechanically. A mechanical harvester works by beating the vine with rubber sticks which knock off the grapes individually on to a conveyor belt. Unfortunately it is not selective in discarding unripe or rotten grapes, and often breaks the skins. For this reason, mechanical harvesting is less widely used for white wines as there is a danger of oxidation. Human pickers cut the whole bunches, with the stalks, off the vine, and can then cut off any unripe or rotten grapes.

It is the quality of the fruit delivered at harvest which is the first important factor in determining the quality of the resultant wine.

CHAPTER TWO

HOW WINE
IS MADE

Wine is, very simply, the fermented juice of grapes. Grapes contain natural sugars which, on contact with yeasts which are found naturally on the fruit skins and in the atmosphere, are converted to alcohol.

The grape is made up of:

Pulp which contains water, sugar, acids and flavouring compounds

Skin which contains colour, tannin and flavouring compounds

Bloom on the oustide of the skin, which contains yeasts and bacteria

Stalks which contain tannin

The ripeness of the grapes is determined by the amount of sugar present. This can be ascertained by measuring the density of the juice; various scales are used, the most common being Beaume and Oechsle. From the reading of the density the potential alcohol of the resulting wine can be calculated. In France, a minimum alcohol level is a requirement for Appellation Contrôlée wines.

Chaptalization is the addition of sugar to the freshly crushed grapes or must to increase the alcohol content of the finished wine. This practice is commonly carried out in cool climates, and can improve the wine if carried out judiciously. It is important to note that the addition of sugar to sweeten a wine is strictly forbidden.

The acids in the grape, principally tartaric and citric, are essential to give the wine balance, but the levels can be increased or decreased. Wines made in cool climates, particularly Germany, often have to be de-acidified, whilst those from warm climates can have their acidity increased, usually by the addition of tartaric or citric acid.

The skins contain the colour and tannins. The juice of most grapes is colourless, so to make red wine the skins must be macerated in the juice to extract the colour pigments. The tannins are tannic acid; this will only be found in red wines, as there is little skin content for white wines. There are also tannins in the stalks, although these are now generally removed prior to fermentation.

Yeasts are found in the bloom on the outside of the grape skin. These consist of both wild yeasts and wine yeasts (*Saccharomyces cerevisiae*). The wild yeasts, and the acetic acid bacteria found on the skins, are killed off by the addition of sulphur dioxide immediately the grapes are brought into the winery. Sulphur dioxide is very important in wine-making, for as well as its anti-septic qualities, it also works as an anti-oxidant, both during the wine-making process and later in the finished wine. However, if used excessively it will give an unpleasant smell and taste to the wine; there are EC limits on the levels allowed.

Fermentation is the conversion of the grape sugars by

yeasts into alcohol; carbon dioxide gas and heat are also produced. As noted above, the wild yeasts are usually killed off by sulphur dioxide, but the wine yeasts will naturally ferment the sugars. However, it is becoming increasingly common for wine-makers to kill off as many of the yeasts as possible and then innoculate the must with specially cultured yeasts, which can influence the style and taste of wine produced, and gives greater control over the fermentation.

Yeasts will die off once all the sugars have been consumed; in any case it is rare for yeasts to survive beyond 15 per cent alcohol. The dead yeast cells will fall to the bottom of the fermentation tank and form a sediment, called lees. Once the alcoholic fermentation is complete, the wine is usually racked off its lees. An exception to this is Muscadet, which is often bottled early straight off the lees, and is described on the label as 'Sur Lie'.

Temperature control during fermentation is critical. Yeasts cannot work if it is too cold, so the must may have to be heated to begin with. Once the fermentation has started, heat is created, so the wine-maker must have the means to cool down the must, either through integral water pipes in the tanks or with a heat-exchanger. The temperature at which a wine is fermented will have an influence on the final taste and style.

The simple process of fermentation has, over centuries, been increasingly developed.

RED WINES

Grapes are brought to the winery in whole bunches if they have been picked by hand, or loose if they have been harvested by machine. For a traditional red wine vinification the grapes are tipped into a crusher/destemmer (*fouloir-egrappoir*). In the past, stalks were often left to macerate in the juice with the skins, but they give extra tannins, which are considered undesirable nowadays. The grape skins are broken by being passed through the wheels of the crusher, and the juice, skins and pips are pumped into the fermentation tanks. Traditional fermentation vats were made of wood, slightly narrower at the top than the bottom, and these are still used, even at the very best estates. However, new wineries today nearly always install stainless steel tanks which are easy to clean. Many older cellars have concrete tanks, lined with glass; the critical factor is that any substance the wine comes into contact with is inert. The tanks are all open at the top to allow the escape of the carbon dioxide gas which is produced during fermentation.

Natural yeasts found in the bloom on the grape skins, as well as in the atmosphere, will immediately start attacking the grape sugars. However, in order to have more control over the course of fermentation, many wineries will add sulphur dioxide to kill off the wild yeasts, and then add a specific quantity of specially cultured yeast. Temperature is critical to the conduct of fermentation – most red wines are fermented between 20 and 35°C. Some wineries heat up the must at the start of fermentation to encourage colour extraction. Conversely, some oenologists recommend cooling the must at the start of fermentation. Maintaining the correct temperature during fermentation has been made much simpler by the use of stainless steel tanks which incorporate water coils in the sides; either hot or cold water can be pumped through as required. With the older wooden and concrete vats, the wine has to be pumped out, passed through a cooling system and then back into the vats.

The second key aspect to red wine production is colour extraction. The grape skins must be kept in contact with the must; nearly all grapes have clear juice – the colour pigments are in the skins. The carbon dioxide gas created during fermentation tends to push the skins to the top of the fermenting wine, forming a cap. This has to be continually submerged with paddles, although some modern fermenting tanks have a grill two-thirds up which prevents the skins from rising higher. Some wine-makers run off part of the juice early in the fermentation, which increases the ratio of skins to juice and therefore leads to greater concentration. This practice, known as *saignée*, is very helpful in less hot years, and the juice run off is not lost; it can be fermented as a rosé wine.

It is also common for the wine to be pumped from the bottom of the tank over the cap during fermentation. This helps colour extraction from the skins as well as reducing the risk of acetic acid bacteria developing. Some wineries have installed rotary fermenters which rotate during fermentation to keep the skins constantly in contact with the juice.

The length of time a red wine will spend on its skins depends very much on the area, grape variety, style of wine and aim of the wine-maker. Much of the colour will be achieved within a week, but wines which require plenty of tannins for long maturation may remain in contact with the skins for two to three weeks. In any case, almost all the sugars will have been fermented within three weeks and it is unusual to keep the wine on its skins once the alcoholic fermentation has finished. The juice is run off from the skins and other solids which are then pumped into a press. The resulting wine, known as *vin de presse*, is very rich in colour and tannin and is kept separate, but some or all may later be blended back with the free-run juice if the wine-maker so desires.

Carbonic maceration

This is a method of whole-berry fermentation which allows colour extraction but with very little tannin. It is a system practised traditionally in the Beaujolais region of France, where the bunches of grapes are tipped, whole and uncrushed, into the fermentation vats and then covered over. The grapes at the bottom are crushed by the weight of those above and start to ferment. Much of the carbon dioxide cannot escape, and, in this atmosphere, the whole grapes start to ferment within their skins, and take on colour but not tannin. After some days, the juice is run off and the grapes are pressed; contrary to the traditional vinification, this press wine is actually less tannic than the free-run wine. It is as a result of this form of vinification that Beaujolais is generally soft and fruity and can be drunk young. This method of wine-making has been developed to ferment whole, uncrushed bunches of grapes placed in sealed tanks which have been filled with carbon dioxide gas. These pure carbonic maceration wines do not age well, but some wine-makers will blend a proportion with traditionally vinified red wine.

ROSÉ WINES

Rosé wine is produced with a short period of skin contact with the black grape skins; usually between one and three days. Many rosés are made from a blend of black and white grapes which are harvested and pressed together. Once the juice has achieved the right degree of colour, it is run off the skins and fermented separately. An increasingly common practice today is the production of rosé wine from black grapes by the *saignée* method mentioned above. The juice is run off the fermenting vats of red wine, between 12 and 24 hours after crushing, and fermented separately in tanks. This enables the producer to increase the concentration of the red wine without losing the juice.

It is illegal, within the EC, to make a rosé by blending red and white wine together. The only exception is champagne; although some producers do ferment the wine after a short period of skin contact with the black grape skins, many add a small amount of still red wine to the blend.

WHITE WINES

Traditionally, white wines are made by pressing the grapes immediately on arrival at the winery. In the past this was usually carried out in vertical basket presses; today most wineries use horizontal presses. The grapes are first crushed, with the stalks left on to facilitate the running of the juice during pressing, then pumped into a press. The horizontal press will either be of the Vaslin type, which consists of two metal plates which converge from each end, slowly squeezing the juice through a slatted cylinder, or the Willmes type, which gives a much gentler press by an inflating rubber bag inside a perforated cylinder.

Skin contact or macération pelliculaire

This is a relatively new practice for white wines. The grape skins contain many flavouring elements which it was felt were being lost: today many wine-makers allow a few hours' contact with the white grape skins at low temperature before pressing. The grapes are both crushed and destalked first, otherwise the tannins from the stalks would taint the wine.

Settling or débourbage

In order to ensure a cleaner fermentation, and as the grape skins have been removed, it is important to clarify the must as much as possible. This is normally done by simply keeping the temperature low to prevent the fermentation from starting, and letting much of the solid matter settle to the bottom of the tank. The cleaned must can then be run off into another tank and the fermentation started. Some wineries use a centrifuge to clean the must prior to fermentation.

The fermentation of white wines is carried out at a lower temperature than for reds – usually between 15 and 20°C, sometimes as low as 10°. The low temperature helps to enhance the fruit flavours and freshness of the wine. However, as fermentation naturally creates heat, temperature control is critical. It is for this reason that the better-equipped modern wineries tend to produce the better white wines. Stainless steel fermentation tanks, with built-in cooling pipes, are almost essential to the production of clean, fresh white wines with good fruit flavours. There is also greater danger of oxidation with white wines than red, so extra care is required throughout the wine-making process.

Vinification of some white wines is still carried out in barrels. In Germany, many of the top estates ferment their wines in large 1000-litre oak casks; the naturally cooler temperature there helps prevent overheating during fermentation. In Burgundy, and many other areas seeking to make fine wines from Chardonnay, as well as Semillon and even Sauvignon grapes, fermentation is carried out in 225-litre oak casks. These will impart a distinctive oak flavour and tannins to the wine, particularly if they are new. The smaller mass of wine will prevent an excessive rise in temperature. The lees will be stirred up during the fermentation to impart extra flavour, and the wine will be racked into another cask as soon as the fermentation has finished.

Malolactic fermentation

This is the conversion by bacteria of malic acid, which is very tart (as in unripe apples), to lactic acid, which is much milder (as in milk). This fermentation can occur at the same time as the alcoholic fermentation, but more often follows it, often in the warmer spring following the vintage; for this reason it was often described as the second fermentation. This reduction in the acidity of the wine is usually sought in red wines and white wines from cool climates. In hotter climates it is often discouraged, as the total acidity levels might be too low for the balance of the wine.

Maturation

The majority of white wines are bottled between 6 months to a year following the vintage. Many red wines, however, because of their concentration and tannins, need time to soften and become more rounded. The best are often aged in casks, usually 225-litre barrels made of oak. The use of new oak casks gives the wine a distinctive vanilla flavour as well as imparting some oak tannins to the wine, but the overall effect is to soften and round out the wine. These flavours diminish with the number of times the barrel is used. In Italy, many red wines are aged in large old casks, which do not impart any wood flavours, but give the wine a distinctive, slightly oxidized character.

Fining

Fining is a means of clarifying a wine by the addition of a substance which will fall through the wine, drawing down any floating particles with it. Quality red wines are usually fined with egg-whites, but isinglass, ox-blood and bentonite are also used.

Filtration

Filtration is the final stage of cleaning a wine prior to bottling. Most wines will be filtered through a plate-filter to remove any remaining particles. Wines which are likely to cause problems in the bottle, such as those with some residual sugar which could re-ferment if stray yeasts were present, will also pass through a very fine membrane filter which will remove any remaining yeast or bacteria. Many producers of fine red wines, which are expected to mature in the bottle and throw a natural sediment, do not filter before bottling, believing that it strips the wine of some of its flavour.

Cold stabilization

Many white wines are refrigerated prior to bottling to ensure tartrate stability. Natural tartaric acid in the wine can precipitate as tartrate crystals if the wine gets very cold when in bottle. By refrigerating before bottling, precipitation of crystals in the bottle will be unlikely. The sugar-like crystals are totally harmless and settle in the bottom of the bottle or glass when poured, so do not necessitate decanting. But there are those who view tartrates in white wines, and sediment in red, as a fault, rather than as a natural occurrence.

Pasteurization

Some wines, particularly red, are pasteurized before bottling as a means of ensuring stability in the bottle, by killing any yeast or bacteria. However, it has to be said that most producers believe it harms the wine.

Bottling

Wines which might be susceptible to problems, such as those with residual sugar, must be bottled in cold sterile conditions, all machinery having been washed through with a solution of dilute sulphur dioxide. Bottles and corks are supplied sterile, although often the bottles are rinsed prior to filling. Hot-bottling is carried out on some everyday wines which ensures stability in the bottle in the same way as pasteurization, but does nothing for the quality of the wine.

Once bottled, all wines require a short period of rest to settle. However, those red wines with high levels of tannin may need years to mature; the tannins will soften in time and the wine will throw a deposit. It is important, therefore, that such wines are correctly stored during their lifetime.

CHAPTER THREE

THE WINES
OF FRANCE

Although Italy can match France in terms of quantity, no other country in the world produces such diversity in the quality of its wine. Favoured by an ideal climate and a wide variety of soils and grapes, the very best French wines remain the benchmark to which most others aspire.

However, it should be noted that nearly half the wine produced in France achieves no quality standard at all. The term **Vin de Table** carries no geographical designation other than Produce of France. These wines, also known as Vins Ordinaires or Vins de Consommation Courante (VCC), used to be the staple drink of the French manual worker, but with wine consumption falling dramatically in France as the result of health awareness campaigns, a large percentage of the wine produced now has to be distilled into industrial alcohol. The system of payment for table wine, by degree of alcohol as well as quantity, encouraged growers to plant very high-yielding grapes, capable of producing high-alcohol wine, in the knowledge that it would never be drunk, but simply sent for distillation. Most Vin de Table comes from the Midi, the southern stretch of the country bordering the Mediterranean.

Vin de Pays was introduced in 1968, as a superior grade of Vin de Table. The aim was to reduce production and improve quality by persuading growers to plant better grape varieties in more suitable sites. Vin de Pays come from delimited areas, which can be regional – Vin de Pays du Jardin de la France, which covers the Loire Valley, Vin de Pays du Comte Tolosan, from south-west France, and Vin de Pays d'Oc from the Midi; or departmental, following the country's administrative 'departments'; or zonal, more restricted, smaller areas, which may have a particular microclimate or soil. In all cases vine varieties and their yields are restricted, minimum alcohol levels are set, and the wines are subject to analytical and tasting tests. A grape variety may be shown on the label.

Vin Délimité de Qualité Supérieure (VDQS) is a quality category introduced in the 1950s which has become a stepping-stone to promotion to full AOC status (see below). Because of this, VDQS wines represent only a very small percentage of total French wine production. The wines have to meet similar restrictions as AOC on grape varieties, yield and alcohol content, and this was the first category that included tasting tests as a requirement.

Appellation d'Origine Contrôlée (AOC) is the primary level of quality control for French wines. The Institut National des Appellations d'Origine was established in 1935 to protect France's most famous vineyards. Areas of production were delimited, grape varieties and vineyard practices specified according to local tradition, yields limited and minimum alcohol levels set, but until 1979 there was no requirement that the wines should be tasted to

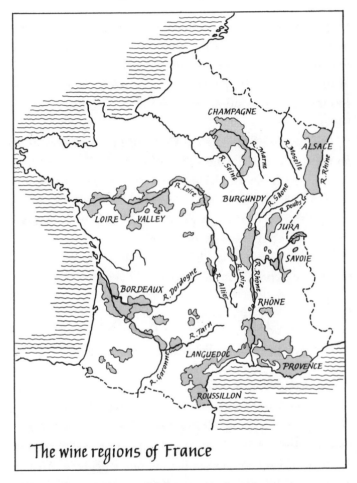

The wine regions of France

achieve AOC status. All of France's best-known wines are AOC, and with the gradual promotion of VDQS wines, there are now over 400 appellations.

It is important to remember, however, that the size of

appellation can vary considerably – for instance, Appellation Bordeaux Contrôlée covers the whole department of the Gironde, whilst Appellation Château Grillet Contrôlée in the Rhône covers a mere 7½ acres. Generally, the more specific the appellation the stricter the controls on the wine.

The system of Appellation Contrôlée is based very much on the origin of the wine and the belief that it is the *terroir*, or soil, which determines the character of the wine. Whilst more and more wines from around the world, including many Vins de Pays from France, are being sold by grape variety, the French authorities have seen fit to ban the use of grape varieties on the labels of Appellation Contrôlée wines, the only exceptions so far being in Alsace and the Loire.

BORDEAUX AND SOUTH-WEST FRANCE

There has been a long historical association between England and Bordeaux ever since the marriage in 1152 of Henry II and Eleanor of Aquitaine brought the vineyard region of Bordeaux into the realm of the English crown. As a result, English, as well as Dutch and French, merchants set up in Bordeaux to trade in the region's wines. The English word claret is derived from a style of wine, *clairet*, a light red or dark rosé, produced in the region.

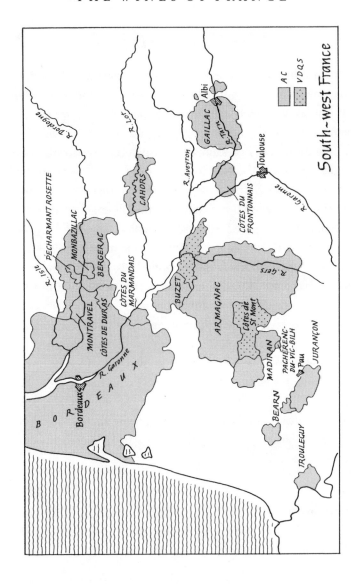

South-west France

AC

VDQS

R. Dordogne

R. Lot

PECHARMANT ROSETTE

MONBAZILLAC

BERGERAC

R. Isle

MONTRAVEL

CÔTES DE DURAS

CÔTES DU MARMANDAIS

CAHORS

R. Aveyron

GAILLAC

R. Tarn

Albi

Toulouse

CÔTES DU FRONTONNAIS

R. Garonne

BUZET

ARMAGNAC

R. Gers

CÔTES DE ST MONT

MADIRAN

PACHERENC-DU-VIC-BILH

Pau

JURANÇON

BÉARN

IROULEGUY

BORDEAUX

Bordeaux

R. Garonne

Négociants-éleveurs

The merchants' traditional role was to buy wine in bulk from the growers of the region, to blend and mature it in their cellars in Bordeaux; hence the term *négociant-éleveur*, meaning a trader who 'brings up' wines. These traders were responsible for the exports of Bordeaux upon which the reputation of the area's wines was built. However, since most wine-growers today age and bottle their wine at the château, the *négociant*'s role is now more that of a middle-man, buying and selling château-bottled wines, as the majority are still only sold through the Bordeaux trade. But most *négociants* do still buy the lesser appellations of the region in bulk to blend and meet the demand for branded and basic generic wines from the supermarkets and major multiple stores.

Most *négociants* will buy wine through a *courtier*, or broker. With over 7000 properties in the region, it is impossible to have an intimate knowledge of every one; a *courtier* may specialize in the wines of a particular area. The *courtier* will present samples and, if the wine is accepted, take a commission from both *negociant* and grower – in return he has to guarantee that the wine delivered matches the sample and the payment.

Climate

Bordeaux lies at the perfect latitude for making great wine. The dominating influences are the Atlantic Ocean and the Dordogne and Garonne rivers, flowing into the Gironde estuary, which create a mild, temperate zone. The region is protected to a degree by pine forests from the prevailing wet westerly winds of the Atlantic but excessive rain and humidity are still problems. An absence of spring frosts, and a good level of sunshine, as well as enough rain to swell the grapes, will be required to produce a great Bordeaux vintage.

Soil

The concept of *terroir*, beloved of the French, is nowhere more closely observed than in the great vineyards of Bordeaux. The eastward movement of the Dordogne and Garonne rivers through to the Gironde estuary over millions of years has left alluvial deposits of sand and gravel on their western banks. The best vineyards of the Médoc and Graves are situated on the higher gravel mounds. In St-Emilion and Pomerol, to the north of the Dordogne river, the vineyards lie either on the limestone escarpment above the river, or on a heavier, more clayey soil on the plateau behind. Between the Dordogne and the Garonne, in the Entre-Deux-Mers (literally, 'between two seas'), the vineyards have a variable mixture of clay and limestone.

Grape varieties

Nearly all Bordeaux wines are a blend of at least two different varieties.

Red wines

Merlot is the most widely planted red variety in the Bordeaux region. It is a thin-skinned grape producing soft, plummy wine, high in alcohol, low in acidity. It blends particularly well with Cabernet-Sauvignon.

Cabernet-Sauvignon likes a cool climate and well-drained soil and is therefore ideally suited to the gravel of the Médoc. Small, thick-skinned grapes produce wines with plenty of tannin and acidity, low in alcohol, but with good colour and a distinctive blackcurranty aroma and flavour.

Cabernet-Franc is similar to Cabernet-Sauvignon but in most cases produces lighter wines with less colour and finesse, although it is particularly suited to the soil in St-Emilion and Pomerol, where it is known as Bouchet.

Petit Verdot produces wine with good colour, tannin and alcohol, but only when fully ripened in hot years.

Malbec also produces highly coloured and tannic wine but is only used by a few properties in a Bordeaux blend.

An average blend in the Médoc would be:
60 per cent Cabernet-Sauvignon
25 per cent Merlot
10 per cent Cabernet-Franc
5 per cent Petit Verdot/Malbec

whilst in St-Emilion it would be:
50 per cent Merlot
50 per cent Cabernet – mostly Franc, but with a little Sauvignon.

In Pomerol the proportion of Merlot would be even higher.

White wines

Sauvignon Blanc is the dominant variety for dry wines; it is generally high in acidity with a distinctive gooseberry aroma. It is often unblended, particularly in Entre-Deux-Mers, but is also found blended in both dry and sweet wines with Semillon.

Semillon is the principal variety for sweet wines; it is thin-skinned and particularly susceptible to *Botrytis cinerea*, or 'noble rot' (see page 6). It has a somewhat fat, lanolin flavour, but, when affected by botrytis, takes on a luscious, honeyed and complex character.

Muscadelle produces flowery, perfumed wines but is only used in very small proportions in some sweet wines.

The 1855 Classification of the Wines of the Gironde

Most of Bordeaux's wines are produced at individual châteaux, which may be no more than simple farms. There are some co-operatives in the region and, as mentioned above, many proprietors sell in bulk to the *négociant-éleveurs*, but more and more producers now age and bottle their wine at the château.

The grandest châteaux, certainly those worthy of the name, were built, mainly in the Médoc, during the seventeenth and eighteenth centuries. For the Exposition Universelle of 1855 in Paris, a classification was made of the top properties of Bordeaux, based on the prices their wines had fetched over the preceding 100 years. The leading 58 red-wine-producing châteaux, which all came from the Médoc, with the exception of Château Haut-Brion in the Graves, were classed in 5 divisions or growths, known as Grands Crus Classés, from Premier down to Cinquième. Although the reputation of many of these châteaux has waxed and waned since 1855, there has been only one official change – the promotion in 1973 of Mouton-Rothschild to Premier Grand Cru Classé.

The sweet wines of Sauternes were also classified in 1855, with Château d'Yquem on its own at the head as Premier Grand Cru, followed by 9 Premiers Crus and 11 Deuxième Crus. The red and white wines of Graves and the wines of St-Emilion were not classified until 100 years later, but these classifications have not carried quite the same importance as that of the Médoc, which, despite the changes in fortune of the different châteaux, is still extensively used.

Some 444 of those châteaux of the Médoc which did not make it to Grand Cru Classé status, were later classified as Crus Bourgeois, although the number has now been reduced to 128. These are generally wines of high quality, and can represent much better value than the more famous Crus Classés. Outside of these classifications, those wines of more modest pretensions, from anywhere in the Bordeaux region, are often referred to as *petits châteaux*. There are some 7000 wine-producing properties in the Gironde, covering around 250,000 acres.

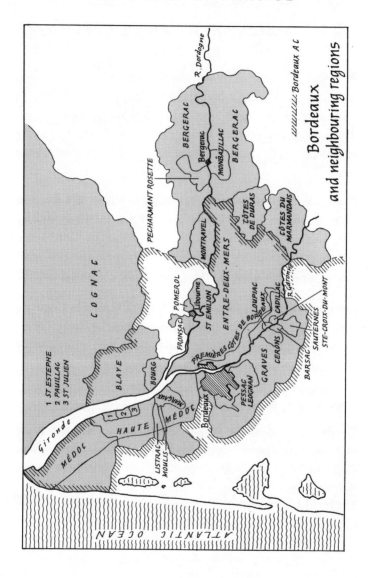

Bordeaux and neighbouring regions

ⅢⅢⅢⅢ Bordeaux AC

R. Dordogne
BERGERAC
Bergerac
MONBAZILLAC
BERGERAC
PECHARMANT ROSETTE
CÔTES DE DURAS
CÔTES DU MARMANDAIS
MONTRAVEL
ENTRE-DEUX-MERS
POMEROL
FRONSAC
Libourne
ST EMILION
Bordeaux
COGNAC
PREMIÈRES CÔTES DE BORDEAUX
R. Garonne
CADILLAC
STE-CROIX-DU-MONT
GRAVES
CÉRONS
SAUTERNES
BARSAC
PESSAC LEOGNAN
BLAYE
BOURG
MARGAUX
Bordeaux
MÉDOC
HAUTE MÉDOC
1 ST ESTEPHE
2 PAUILLAC
3 ST JULIEN
1 2 3
Gironde
LISTRAC
MOULIS
MÉDOC
ATLANTIC OCEAN

43

The Bordeaux Appellations Contrôlées
Red wines

Bordeaux Rouge   The simple appellation for the region; the wines will usually be predominantly Merlot, but with some Cabernet-Franc and Cabernet-Sauvignon. Often, these wines are sold as house claret, but there are many well-made individual châteaux wines, which offer better value.

Bordeaux Supérieur   Similar wines but with 0.5 per cent more alcohol; usually worth seeking out in preference to straight Bordeaux.

Appellations between the Dordogne and Garonne:

Ste-Foy-Bordeaux, **Graves de Vayres**, **Premières Côtes de Bordeaux**   Individual appellations within the Entre-Deux-Mers; the latter, particularly, will usually have a little more depth and concentration than basic Bordeaux.

Appellations north of the Dordogne:

Bordeaux   Côtes de Francs and **Côtes de Castillon** are two areas to the east of St-Emilion which produce good-quality wines.

Lussac, Puisséguin, Montagne and **St-Georges** are villages lying to the north of St-Emilion which can add its name to theirs, e.g. Lussac St-Emilion. The wines are lighter; usually a 50/50 blend of Merlot and Cabernet.

St-Emilion The best wines are the 11 châteaux classified as Premier Grand Cru Classé, notably Château Cheval Blanc and Château Ausone, which were accorded special recognition as a separate Class A. There are also 63 châteaux classified as Grand Cru. The production under this appellation is as large as the 6 village appellations in the Médoc put together.

Pomerol Many of the finest Merlot-dominated wines are produced in this small appellation; a plateau bordering St-Emilion with a soil rich in iron oxide. Although the wines have never been classified, Château Pétrus now achieves prices well above the first growths of the Médoc, and several others can match those of the other leading classified growths.

Fronsac, Canon-Fronsac, Lalande de Pomerol Principally Merlot-based wines, but without the concentration of Pomerol, although the first two areas are very much on an upward quality curve, and are becoming increasingly sought after.

Côtes de Bourg, Premières Côtes de Blaye Two areas north of Bordeaux, at the confluence of the Dordogne and Garonne rivers. Generally modest wines, although the best are certainly above basic Bordeaux quality.

Appellations west of the Garonne:

Graves and **Pessac-Leognan** lie to the south of Bordeaux.

Graves takes its name from the gravelly soil of the area, and the wines are made predominantly from Cabernet, both Sauvignon and Franc. Thirteen châteaux were classified in 1959 for red wine and 8 for white. Pessac-Leognan is an appellation introduced in 1987 which covers the area just to the south of Bordeaux itself, and includes all the classified growths.

Médoc This appellation covers the northern end of the peninsula on the western bank of the Gironde estuary. The large masses of water either side help to regulate the temperature and provide an almost ideal temperate climate. Although the wines are generally not as concentrated as those from the Haut-Médoc there are some excellent Crus Bourgeois.

Haut-Médoc covers the southern end of the Médoc peninsula. This is the district from which the classed growths of 1855 come (with the exception of Haut-Brion) and 5 fall within this appellation. The best vineyards lie on banks of siliceous gravel, and the Cabernet-Sauvignon grape dominates.

There are 6 individual village appellations which represent the apogée of fine Bordeaux red wine. Running northwards from Bordeaux, these are:

Margaux (with 21 Crus Classés and one Premier Cru)
Moulis
Listrac
St-Julien (11 Crus Classés)

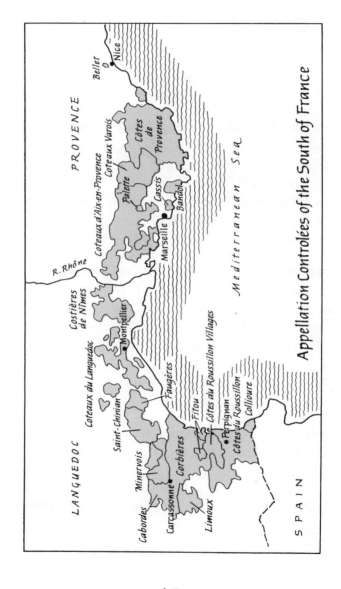

Appellation Controlées of the South of France

Pauillac (18 Crus Classés, including 3 Premiers Crus)
St-Estèphe (5 Crus Classés)

White wines
DRY

Bordeaux Blanc is usually a blend of Sauvignon and Semillon. This appellation is used to encompass some very ordinary, often highly sulphured, off-dry white wines. The increased demand for dry white wines helped to stimulate major changes in viticultural and wine-making practices, with the result that there are now many clean, fresh and dry white wines sold under the appellation.

Entre-Deux-Mers Bordeaux's largest district, covering the apex between the Dordogne and Garonne. It is here that the results of the white Bordeaux revolution are best seen – many of the vines are wider-spaced and trained high, and cool fermentation has produced wines with more aroma and freshness. Many of the wines sold under this appellation are made from 100 per cent Sauvignon Blanc and therefore taste crisper, with more bite.

Graves has a better reputation for its red than its white wines. Historically, white Graves was often medium-sweet and over-sulphured. Today there are many properties producing excellent wines, usually quite full-flavoured, as a result of being made predominantly from Semillon, barrel-fermented.

SWEET

Premières Côtes de Bordeaux, **Cadillac**, **Loupiac** and **Ste-Croix-du-Mont** are sweet white wine appellations, lying on the north bank of the Garonne, south of Bordeaux. These wines are generally light, although the best, particularly Loupiac and Ste-Croix-du-Mont, are made with a certain proportion of grapes affected by botrytis (see below). The prices these wines fetch, unlike those produced on the southern bank of the Gironde, do not justify several pickings.

Cerons is a small appellation on the south bank of the Garonne within the Graves district, producing modestly priced sweet wines, similar to those north of the river.

Sauternes and **Barsac** are without doubt the most complex sweet wines, particularily in years when the grapes have been affected by 'noble rot'. This fungal growth, *Botrytis cinerea*, develops on the grape skins during the autumn, encouraged by the humidity created by damp mornings and warm, dry afternoons. The effect is to allow much of the liquid in the grape to evaporate, thereby concentrating the sugars and acids. The yield is much reduced, and, as the grapes are infected individually, pickers may have to pass through the vineyard six or eight times during the harvest; each picking is called a *trie*. *Botrytis cinerea* does not develop every year and when it occurs it will be to varying degrees, but in those years when the vines have been fully affected, the resulting wine will be lusciously sweet, as well as reading 14–15 per cent alcohol.

Such wines are invariably expensive, as the yields will obviously be much smaller: fermentation can be very difficult with such high levels of sugar, and the best wines will be matured in new oak casks.

Other wines from South-west France

The region of Bergerac is a continuation of the Bordeaux vineyards eastwards along the Dordogne river. The red wines are much in the style of the St-Emilion satellites, made from a blend of Merlot and Cabernet (predominantly Franc). The basic appellation is **Bergerac**; **Côtes de Bergerac** indicates only a degree higher alcohol. **Pécharmant** is a small appellation producing generally fuller and better wines. The dry whites, **Bergerac** or **Montravel**, are usually Sauvignon-based but can also be blended with Semillon. **Côtes de Bergerac Blanc**, **Côtes de Montravel**, **Haut-Montravel** and **Rosette** are always *moelleux* (sweet). **Saussignac** and **Monbazillac** are small areas exclusively with appellations for sweet white wine often made from late-picked and even botrytized grapes.

Côtes de Buzet, **Côtes de Duras** and **Côtes du Marmandais** lie to the south of Bergerac and produce red and dry white wines in the mould of the lesser, and lighter, Bordeaux appellations. The reds are generally more interesting.

Cahors used to be called the 'black wine', made as it is predominantly from the Malbec grape. The style now is somewhat lighter, but still with a full, plummy fruit flavour.

Gaillac, lying to the west of Albi, produces light, fruity reds, predominantly from the Duras grape, and a whole host of white wines. Gaillac Blanc is made from a blend of grapes, including Sauvignon, Mauzac and the local Len de l'el; it is often produced as Sec Perlé, with a small amount of carbonic gas. It can also be sweet (*Doux, Liquoreux* or *Moelleux*), or sparkling (*Mousseux*).

Côtes du Frontonnais Medium-bodied, fruity reds and rosés from at least 60 per cent of Negrette grapes.

Madiran Rich, tannic wines made with at least 40 per cent of Tannat grapes.

Jurançon, in the foothills of the Pyrenees, has long been famous for its sweet wines produced primarily from over-ripened Gros and Petit Manseng grapes, although a lot is now made into dry white wine.

Limoux is best known for its sparkling Crémant, previously known as Blanquette, but it is also an appellation for dry white wine. In the past it was predominantly made from the local Mauzac grape, but more and more Chardonnay has been introduced. As from the 1992 vintage – uniquely under the Appellation Contrôlée regime – Limoux must be wholly barrel-fermented.

Côtes de Gascogne is simply a Vin de Pays from the Armagnac region, where many growers have turned from brandy to wine production. Generally light, fruity whites from Ugni Blanc and Colombard, these wines have become extremely popular.

BURGUNDY AND EASTERN FRANCE

Burgundy is usually compared to Bordeaux in arguments about which region produces the greatest red wines, but there can be little doubt that it is from Burgundy that France's greatest dry white wines come. However, the total production of Burgundy is only half that of Bordeaux, and 60 per cent of it comes from the Beaujolais.

The area differs considerably from Bordeaux in that, rather than being made up of single properties or châteaux with an individual owner, each vineyard often belongs to many different smallholders. Much of the area was in the hands of the Church prior to the Revolution; the lack of wealth in the region meant that, when the land was auctioned after seizure, it became fragmented, and this has been exacerbated by inheritance laws which have reduced the size of landholdings even further. There are now 12,000 growers in the department of the Côte d'Or with an average holding of just one acre.

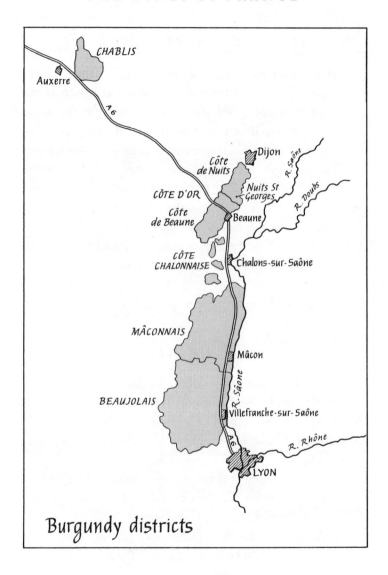

Burgundy districts

Négociants *and growers*

With this proliferation of smallholders the role of the *négociant*, buying and blending wines from several different owners, has been extremely important, particularly during the nineteenth century as exports developed with improved transport. However, over the last 25 years more and more growers have taken to bottling their own wines, partly as a result of the equipment becoming more accessible, but also as a consequence of a few well-publicized frauds during the 1950s and 1960s. It is, however, unrealistic to assume that all *négociants'* wines are inferior; many of the best *négociants* are themselves important vineyard owners with impeccably run estates.

The region of Burgundy encompasses 5 very distinct areas:

Chablis

This is the most northerly district, centred around the town of Chablis and isolated from the rest of Burgundy, 100 km north-west of the Côte d'Or. The northerly situation and continental climate can lead to frost problems, especially in the spring.

The soil is made up of calcareous clay, particularly of the Kimmeridgian type, which is considered by many growers to give Chablis its individual character.

There are 4 Chablis appellations, all for white wine produced from Chardonnay grapes. This variety thrives on chalky soils in a cool climate, producing wines with body and the capacity to age.

The appellation **Chablis Grand Cru** applies to the wines produced from the 7 finest vineyards, which are all situated on one hill just to the north-east of the town of Chablis. A further 12 vineyards scattered within the Chablis appellation are entitled to be classified as **Chablis Premier Cru**. By far the largest quantity of wine is produced under the simple village **Chablis** appellation. The lowest appellation is **Petit Chablis**, although only small quantities are produced, mostly from outlying vineyards.

The quintessential style of Chablis is a crisp, steely Chardonnay with a pronounced acidity. However, most growers are now ensuring that the wines undergo a malolactic fermentation, and many are putting their wines, certainly the Premier and Grand Cru, in oak, to give a fuller, more rounded flavour.

Sauvignon de St-Bris is only a VDQS rather than Appellation Contrôlée wine, but is none the less a good-quality white wine made, uniquely for Burgundy, from the Sauvignon grape in an area to the west of Chablis, around the village of St-Bris-le-Vineux.

The Côte d'Or

Côte de Nuits

The northern end of the Côte d'Or takes its name from the town of Nuits St-Georges. The vineyards run in a narrow strip, on easterly-facing slopes, from just south of Dijon to just north of Beaune. The soil is limestone overlaid with marl and scree, becoming more alluvial at the bottom of the slopes.

The Côte de Nuits produces almost exclusively red wine, made solely from the Pinot Noir grape. This variety needs a temperate climate with a long growing season in a warm, rich and reasonably moist soil. This is the most northerly and coolest region in France in which great red wine is made.

Grand Cru, Premier Cru and village wines

The Côte de Nuits has 22 of Burgundy's 23 red **Grand Cru** vineyards. These have been recognized as producing the finest wines in Burgundy and are designated with their own Appellation Contrôlée. They have only to show the vineyard name on the label – for example, Chambertin, Echézeaux, Romanée-Conti. In Burgundy the term Grand Cru is totally different to the Grands Crus Classés of Bordeaux, which are wholly outside the system of Appellation Contrôlée. The consumer can be further confused because most of the Grand Cru vineyards in Burgundy have several owners – one of the largest, Clos de Vougeot, has 85 owners of its 120 acres. Many of the growers make and bottle their own wine, resulting in great variations in style and quality, even when the wine is made from the same vinestock grown on the same soil.

Next down the hierarchy come the **Premier Cru**

vineyards, whose names follow the village name on the label; for example, Gevrey-Chambertin Les Cazetiers, Vosne-Romanée Les Suchots. These vineyards do not generally produce such great wine as the Grands Crus, but are sufficiently superior to be distinguished from a simple village wine.

Then follow the straight village appellations. Running south from Dijon, they are Fixin, Gevrey-Chambertin, Morey St-Denis, Chambolle-Musigny, Vougeot, Vosne-Romanée and Nuits St-Georges. An understanding of the numerous appellations in Burgundy is not helped by the fact that many of Burgundy's villages have added the name of their finest vineyard to their own!

At either end of the Côte, the vineyards are only entitled to the humbler appellation of Côte de Nuits Villages, while the area on top and to the west of the Côte has the appellation of Hautes Côtes de Nuits. Nevertheless, these wines, when well made by a conscientious grower, can offer very good-value drinking.

In years with sufficiently hot, sunny summers, the Côte de Nuits produces firm, full-bodied red wines, with a distinctive fruit and vegetal flavour that is the character of Pinot Noir. Only in the very hottest years will the wines have the tannins found in Bordeaux, and consequently Burgundy will nearly always mature sooner than claret. At Grand Cru level, and when made by one of the top domaines, these rank among the finest French red wines.

Les Chevaliers du Tastevin

This *confrérie*, or brotherhood, was established in the 1930s to promote Burgundy's image. It is best known for the large dinners held in the Château of Clos de Vougeot, for which members dress in colourful medieval robes. But, more importantly, the *confrérie* is also responsible for the award of the Tastevinage label for wines submitted at an annual tasting, and this can be a useful guide for the consumer.

Côte de Beaune

The Côte de Beaune, the southern end of the Côte d'Or, runs in a south-westerly direction from north of Beaune as far as Chagny. Its slopes appear slightly gentler than the Côte de Nuits, of which it is a natural continuation.

The area has a more temperate but slightly wetter climate than the Côte de Nuits. The soil of this limestone ridge is similar to that of the Côte de Nuits, but there are significant outcrops of calcareous, light clay, particularly at Meursault and Puligny, and this is where the Chardonnay grape takes over from the Pinot Noir.

The red wines, again exclusively from Pinot Noir, tend to be lighter and softer in style than those of the Côte de Nuits, but the best, from Aloxe-Corton, Beaune, Pommard and Volnay make up for it in finesse.

It is, however, the white Chardonnay wines of the Côte de Beaune that are considered among the finest dry white wines of France. Seven of Burgundy's 8 Grand Cru white wines come from the Côte de Beaune. Apart from Corton-Charlemagne, in the village of Aloxe-Corton, north of Beaune, the remaining Grands Crus come from the villages of Puligny and Chassagne-Montrachet, Montrachet itself being considered by many as the greatest dry white wine in the world. The village of Meursault, whilst not having any Grand Crus, is perhaps better known for its rich, buttery, nutty Chardonnay.

The Côte de Beaune is also a source of more reasonably priced Burgundy, both red and white, from less well-known villages such as Savigny-Les-Beaune, Chorey-Les-Beaune, Monthélie, St-Aubin and Santenay.

The **Côte de Beaune** appellation is reserved for wines produced just around Beaune, whilst **Côte de Beaune Villages** can come from anywhere on the Côte, but only from red grapes.

Hautes Côtes de Beaune comes from the higher slopes above and to the west of the Côte itself. These generic appellations of the Côte de Beaune are more widely seen than those from the Côte de Nuits, and again often offer good value.

The Hospices de Beaune

The magnificent Hôtel-Dieu, with its exquisitely tiled roof, is the home of the Hospices de Beaune, a charitable institution established in the fifteenth century to care for the sick and poor. Over 130 acres of vineyards have been bequeathed to the Hospices, who tend the vines and make the wine, which is then auctioned in cask during the third week of November following the harvest.

Because of the charitable status of the Hospices, the prices of its wines tend to be high, but they are a good indicator for a particular vintage. The wines are labelled with the distinctive Hospices label, although there can be differences between bottles as a result of the variable storage and bottling conditions among the *négociants* who have bought individual casks.

Côte Chalonnaise

The Côte Chalonnaise lies to the south of the Côte d'Or, but is not a continuation of it, rather a collection of small groups of hills to the west of the town of Chalon-sur-Saône.

The climate is slightly drier than that of the Côte d'Or to the north and the region is less affected by problems of frost and hail. The Côte Chalonnaise has a limestone subsoil similar to that of the Côte d'Or, but with a sandy clay topsoil.

The principal grape varieties are again Pinot Noir for red wine and Chardonnay for white, but with an important production of Aligote. This white grape variety with a pronounced acidity is grown throughout Burgundy on sites unsuitable for Chardonnay. Aligote was the wine chosen by Canon Kir of Dijon to add to Crème de Cassis to make the aperitif that bears his name, the acidity of the white wine perfectly complementing the sweet blackcurrant liqueur. The village of Bouzeron, just south of Chagny at the northern end of the Côte Chalonnaise, is the only village appellation exclusive to Aligote; all other wines from this grape bear the simple appellation **Bourgogne Aligote**.

The appellations of **Rully**, **Mercurey** and **Givry** are for both red and white wines, whilst **Montagny** at the southern end of the Côte has an appellation exclusively for white. These wines offer good value in Burgundy, for while they may not have the depth and concentration of those from the Côte d'Or, they still show good varietal character at a much lower price.

The Mâconnais

The Maconnais covers a large area west of the river Saône, from Tournus in the north to south of Mâcon, and west to Cluny. The area is made up of soft rolling hills, with mixed agriculture, except at the southern end where there are steeper and more dramatic hills around Pouilly-Fuisse. The soil is predominantly clay over a limestone subsoil but with a greater outcrop of limestone scree in the south.

Two-thirds of the production is white wine from Chardonnay; a quarter is red from the Gamay grape of Beaujolais, with a small amount of red coming from Pinot Noir.

The basic appellation is **Mâcon**, both red and white, produced mostly in the northern area. **Mâcon Supérieur** indicates one degree more alcohol.

Mâcon Villages is an appellation reserved for white wines from Chardonnay grown in 42 villages, which are entitled to substitute their name with Villages on the label; the best-known are Lugny, Viré and Clesse. The best of these wines can match some of the village wines of the Côte d'Or, and offer among the best-value Chardonnay wines from Burgundy.

St-Véran and Pouilly-Fuisse are two small areas, bordering the Beaujolais, with their own appellations, which, at their best, offer a greater concentration of flavour than Mâcon Villages. Both are exclusively white from Chardonnay, and Pouilly-Fuisse should not be confused with Pouilly-Fumé from the Loire. Pouilly-Fuisse has tended to be somewhat overpriced in recent years due to its great popularity, particularly in the United States. Pouilly-Vinzelles and Pouilly-Loche are two neighbouring but much smaller appellations.

The Beaujolais

The most southerly district of the Burgundy region, covering an area just sound of Mâcon to north of Lyon, extending westwards from the river Saône, Beaujolais is also the most individual. In terms of climate, soil, grape variety, viticulture and wine-making it has little in common with other Burgundy wines. Beaujolais produces nearly two-thirds of all Burgundy.

The climate is much more influenced by the Mediterranean than the rest of Burgundy; it is sunnier but also more prone to sudden rainy storms. The northern part of the district is made up of granite hills, with a schistous topsoil of granite and clay. The southern area is flatter with a limestone/clay soil mixture.

The grape variety for red Beaujolais, which accounts for 99 per cent of the production, is the Gamay. It produces its finest wines when grown in granitic soils; these wines are full of fruit, quite high in acidity but with characteristic freshness. The vines of the southern Beaujolais are largely devoted to the production of **Beaujolais Primeur** or **Nouveau**, which accounts for half the sales of all Beaujolais.

The Gamay vines are not trained on wires, but grown as bushes, *en gobelet*. The grapes are not crushed prior to fermentation but tipped into the vats in whole bunches, where they undergo a partial carbonic maceration. This results in a much lower tannin extraction and enhances the fruit flavours, with the result that it is possible to market the wine by the third week of November following the harvest – the traditional release date for Beaujolais Primeur or Nouveau. The better wines from the northern hills are more likely to be vinified traditionally and aged in oak *foudres* prior to bottling.

The most simple appellation is **Beaujolais**, most of which is produced in the southern area. **Beaujolais Supérieur** indicates one degree extra alcohol. **Beaujolais Villages** may only come from 38 villages, mostly in the northern hills, which can also show the name of the individual village instead of the collective Villages.

However, the finest wines are known as the **Cru Beaujolais**. These are produced in 10 villages which show only their own name on the label and do not indicate the term Beaujolais at all. They are: Brouilly, Côte de Brouilly, Chénas, Chiroubles, Fleurie, Juliénas, Morgon, Moulin à Vent, Régnie, St-Amour. Brouilly covers the largest area, Moulin à Vent is considered the fullest and longest-lived; Fleurie is the best-known and perhaps most atypical Cru.

A minute quantity of **Beaujolais Blanc** is produced from Chardonnay grapes.

The lesser appellations of Burgundy

Bourgogne Passetoutgrains, a blend of Gamay with at least one-third Pinot Noir grapes, is often grown, particularly in the Côte d'Or, on soil unsuitable or disallowed for Pinot Noir. The wine has the fruity character of Gamay when young and good examples can develop true Pinot Noir flavour with age.

Bourgogne Grande Ordinaire, red, white or rosé, can be a blend of any of the grape varieties allowed in Burgundy, but is not normally worth seeking out.

Bourgogne Rouge and **Blanc** must be produced from Pinot Noir and Chardonnay respectively and can be very fine, especially when made by a quality-conscious grower in the Côte d'Or.

Jura and Savoie

The Jura mountains lie to the east of Burgundy's Côte d'Or, with vineyards on the lower slopes. The basic appellation of **Côtes de Jura** covers red and rosé wines from Pinot Noir and the local Poulsard and Trousseau grapes, and white from Chardonnay and the local Savagnin. **Arbois** is a smaller appellation around the town of the same name.

Jura is best known, however, for its **Vin Jaune**, a white wine from the Savagnin grape, which is left in casks for 6 years after fermentation, without topping up. The resultant oxidation, and the development of *flor*, a yeast film covering the wine, gives it a unique character, not unlike a Fino sherry, but unfortified and with much higher acidity.

Château Chalon, a small appellation within the Côtes de Jura, is considered to produce the finest Vin Jaune.

Savoie is well known to those who ski in the area. The appellation **Vin de Savoie** covers red, white and rosé wines, the whites, particularly the well-known **Apremont**, one of several villages with the right to add their name, being the best. **Crépy** is a small appellation bordering Lake Geneva which produces good white wine from Chasselas grapes.

THE RHÔNE AND SOUTHERN FRANCE

The vineyards of the Rhône Valley stretch from just south of Lyon as far as Avignon. However, the region divides into two distinct districts: the northern Rhône consists of a narrow strip of vines following the river from Vienne south to Montélimar; the southern Rhône covers a much broader spread of vineyards from Montélimar to Avignon and eastwards into Haute-Provence.

The Northern Rhône

The climate here is more continental than Mediterranean, although the influence of the *mistral*, the violent, cold wind of Provence, is often felt, and vineyards are protected from it by lines of poplar and cypress trees. The soil is primarily granitic, mixed with sandstone on the steep banks along the river, and with more clay in the vineyards lying further back.

The only red grape variety allowed is Syrah, although even for red wines it is often blended with the permitted white varieties of Viognier, Marsanne and Roussanne.

The principal appellations running south from Vienne are:

Côte-Rôtie with its steep, terraced vineyards on the right bank of the river around the town of Ampuis, produces a full, deep-coloured, concentrated red wine from Syrah, but with 20 per cent white Viognier grapes allowed. There are two separate areas of Côte-Rôtie, known as Côte Brune with a clay/iron-rich soil and Côte Blonde with a chalk/clay soil. The wines are sometimes sold as coming from one part of the appellation or as a blend of the two. The firm of E. Guigal has been in the vanguard of promoting the

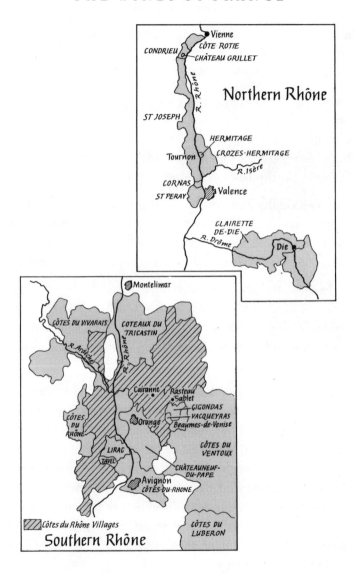

reputation of Côte-Rôtie, particularly with its single-vineyard wines, which fetch prices above those achieved by Bordeaux's Premiers Grands Crus Classés.

Condrieu is a full-bodied, dry white wine with a distinctive floral aroma, made from the Viognier grape. This variety is difficult to grow, ripens late and has a low yield, but it is being increasingly planted in the south of France because of the rich, peachy-flavoured wines it produces.

Château Grillet lies within the Condrieu appellation and is a very similar wine, also from the Viognier. Its rarity as one of the smallest, and the only single-estate, Appellations Contrôlées in France has meant that it is somewhat overpriced.

St-Joseph covers a large area along the right bank of the Rhône from Condrieu right down to Valence. Red wines are produced from Syrah, with up to 10 per cent Marsanne or Roussanne; white wines solely from Marsanne and Roussanne. Both are lighter versions of Hermitage.

Hermitage is the best-known appellation of the northern Rhône. The vines are grown on an impressive hill on the left bank of the river, with an ideal, southerly exposure. The red wines from Syrah, with up to 15 per cent Marsanne or Roussanne, are deeply coloured, full-bodied, with a spicy, rich, blackcurrant fruit flavour. Hermitage from one of the top producers is rightly considered one of the great, classic French red wines. White Hermitage, from Marsanne and Roussanne, is a dry, full-bodied, fragrantly fruity wine, but rarely in the same league as the red.

Crozes-Hermitage is a large appellation by the standards of the northern Rhône, covering the lower-lying areas surrounding Hermitage. It is made from the same grape varieties, but on a heavier, more clayey soil. The wines tend to be lighter and somewhat coarser than Hermitage itself, and mature sooner.

Cornas is a small appellation just north of Valence on the right bank. A red wine, made from 100 per cent Syrah, it is very dark, tannic, full-bodied and needs a long time to mature.

St-Peray is a white wine from Marsanne and Roussanne grown across the river from Valence. It can also be made into a Mousseux, by bottle-fermentation.

Clairette de Die is a sparkling wine made by bottle-fermentation south-east of Valence, from at least 75 per cent Clairette grapes, with the balance Muscat. Clairette de Die Tradition must have at least 50 per cent Muscat, with the balance Clairette, and is the closest France gets to Asti Spumante.

The Southern Rhône

This large area accounts for 95 per cent of the total production of the whole Côtes du Rhône region. The climate here is definitely Mediterranean, with olive trees, lavender and the *maquis* as well as vineyards. The subsoil is mainly limestone, with clay, sand and particularly stony topsoil. The vineyards of **Châteauneuf du Pape** are famous for their large, rounded boulders covering a red alluvial soil, a legacy of glacial movement down the Rhône valley.

A diversity of grape varieties are allowed in the wines of the southern Rhône, but Grenache is the dominant red type. It produces wines high in alcohol with a sweet, spicy fruit flavour.

Côtes du Rhône is the simplest appellation, which, although covering the whole region, in fact comes almost entirely from the south. It can vary from a very modest blend to a good-quality single-domaine wine. The reds and rosés come mainly from Grenache, with Syrah, Mourvèdre, Carignan and Cinsault; the whites from Clairette, Roussanne and Bourboulenc are generally less interesting.

Côtes du Rhône Villages is a superior appellation covering 17 villages, all in the southern Rhône, which have the right to add their name to the appellation. The regulations for the red and rosé wines specify a maximum of 65 per cent Grenache, a minimum of 25 per cent Syrah, Mourvèdre and Cinsault, and 10 per cent total maximum of other varieties; for the whites, a minimum of 80 per cent Clairette, Roussanne and Bourboulenc, 10 per cent Grenache Blanc and maximum 10 per cent of other varieties. Côtes du Rhône Villages is more full-bodied than simple Côtes du Rhône – the regulations stipulate 12½ per cent minimum alcohol rather than 11 per cent for Côtes du Rhône – with more depth and character. The overall quality is higher than Côtes du Rhône, particularly at the generic level.

Vacqueyras has recently been upgraded from a Côtes du Rhône Villages to its own appellation, although its wines are not necessarily better than some of the other villages.

Gigondas, east of Orange, produces red and rosé wines from up to 80 per cent Grenache. The reds are deeply coloured with a full, rich flavour, very similar in style to Châteauneuf du Pape, and generally offering better value.

Châteaneuf du Pape is easily the best-known wine of the Rhône. The village takes its name from the time of the dual papacy when Avignon became the home of the Pope in exile from Rome. The system of Appellation Contrôlée had its beginnings here as a result of the efforts in the 1930s of Baron le Roy, owner of Château Fortia, one of the leading estates, to ensure the standards and reputation of the name. In fact the appellation regulations have a unique require-ment that between 5 per cent and 20 per cent of the grapes are eliminated at harvest from the Appellation Contrôlée wine, to ensure that unripe and damaged grapes are excluded; a process known as *rape*.

The vineyards cover a large area between Orange and Avignon and are renowned for the large stones which absorb heat during the day and then release it at night, thus giving the grapes an extended ripening period. However, there are significant variations in the soil over the appellation, which results in varying styles of wine. Furthermore, up to 13 different grape varieties, 8 red and 5 white, are allowed, although in practice most producers might use 6: a typical composition for the red wine would be 40 per cent Grenache, 30 per cent Syrah, 20 per cent Cinsault and Mourvèdre, with Cunoise and Terret Noir making up the rest. The wines tend to be rich and full-bodied, with a warm, spicy fruit flavour, and high in alcohol – a minimum of 12½ per cent! There is a small but much appreciated production of white Châteauneuf du Pape which tends to be full-flavoured, rich and dry.

Lirac lies on the opposite bank of the Rhône, with gravel and stones overlying sand and red alluvial soil. The appellation allows red, white and rosé wines, but it is the reds which are most interesting, made with a minimum of 40 per cent Grenache plus Cinsault, Mourvèdre and Syrah.

Tavel, just to the south of Lirac, is the best-known dry French rosé wine. The wine is made from blending red and white grapes – Cinsault, Grenache, Carignan, Clairette, Picpoul and Bourboulenc – which are crushed together and then pumped into vats. The skins are removed after 12 hours and the wine must reach a minimum of 11 per cent alcohol. The wine is dry and full-bodied, with a fragrantly fruity aroma.

Muscat de Beaumes de Venise is an appellation for Vin Doux Naturel, a sweet, fortified wine made from the Muscat grape. The fermentation is stopped at 5 per cent alcohol by the addition of pure grape spirit, a process known as *mutage*. The wine retains a minimum of 110 grams per litre of grape sugars at 15 per cent alcohol. The colour can vary from golden-yellow to pale pink, but the essence of the wine is its flowery aroma and honeyed flavour.

Rasteau is another Vin Doux Naturel but is made from the Grenache grape; mostly red, although it can be white or rosé, it has never achieved the popularity of Beaumes de Venise.

Coteaux du Tricastin is an appellation on the east bank of the river between Montélimar and Bollène. The red wines in particular can be very good, especially those with a good proportion of Syrah in the blend.

Côtes du Ventoux, to the east of Avignon, produces red, white and rosé wines grown on a limestone soil. The red wines are again the most interesting, being generally lighter versions of Côtes du Rhône.

Côtes du Luberon produces good-quality red, white and rosé wines.

Provence

The vineyards of Provence stretch eastwards from the Rhône delta almost as far as the Italian border. The region is best known for its rosé wines sold in curved, fluted bottles, which account for 60 per cent of its production. However, it is the reds which are now becoming more seriously appreciated.

The climate is typically hot with warm winters – vintages

do not vary significantly. There is a wide variety of soil types with limestone and granite being the most dominant. The grape varieties grown are much the same as in the southern Rhône.

Coteaux d'Aix en Provence is a large appellation for red, white and rosé wines stretching north and west of Aix-en-Provence itself. Many estates have replanted and included Cabernet-Sauvignon, but the maximum now allowed in a blend for the red wine is 30 per cent.

Côtes de Provence covers an even larger area east of Marseille almost as far as Cannes. Whilst there is an easy local market for its rosé wines, leading estates are producing much more interesting red wines from Grenache, Syrah, Mourvèdre, Cinsault and also a little Cabernet-Sauvignon.

Bandol, on the coast just to the west of Toulon, produces very high-quality red wines, predominantly from the Mourvèdre grape. This variety gives good colour, spicy, plum fruit flavours and tannin, making it a wine that needs a degree of maturity. The white and rosé wines of the appellation are generally not in the same league.

Cassis, to the east of Marseille, is best known for its white wine, made from Ugni Blanc, Clairette and, unusually, Sauvignon Blanc, but its relatively small production has made it over-priced.

Palette is a tiny appellation just south-east of Aix-en-

Provence, three-quarters of which is owned by one estate, Château Simone, producing red, white and rosé wines.

Bellet is a small outpost of an appellation, north of Nice, whose fragrant, dry white wines are especially good.

Coteaux Varois and **Coteaux de Pierrevert** are two VDQS regions in central Provence.

Languedoc-Roussillon

This region, often referred to as the Midi, covers the area westwards from the Rhône delta to the Spanish border, and produces roughly one-third of all the wine in France, albeit mostly bulk Vin de Table of little quality. However, over the last 10 to 15 years, with French Government and EC assistance, many growers have replanted their vineyards with better grape varieties, reduced yields and invested in modern cellar equipment.

The warm climate and rich alluvial soil of the plains bordering the Mediterranean lend themselves to the easy cultivation of high-yielding grape varieties, most of which end up in anonymous blends in the local co-operatives. However, the better vineyards lie on limestone or granite soils on the hillsides.

The Carignan is the dominant red grape of the Languedoc-Roussillon, and is the most widely planted variety in France. It can be high-yielding, dull and coarse, but when it is severely pruned, particularly on old vines, it produces wines with good colour and body and becomes an important part of a blend.

Roughly 90 per cent of France's Vins de Pays (see pages 33–4) come from the Languedoc. They may be restricted to a small area (such as Vin de Pays des Sables du Golfe du Lion), a department (as in Vin de Pays de l'Aude) or a region (Vin de Pays d'Oc covers the whole of Languedoc/Roussillon and Provence). The regulations are exactly the same, and the quality of some domaine-bottled wines is often extremely high. Overall, Vins de Pays usually offer extremely good value for money.

The principal appellations in the Languedoc are:

Coteaux du Languedoc is a large appellation for red and rosé wines covering several different areas, the best villages of which may add their own name (La Clape is the best known).

Costières de Nîmes, south-east of the Roman city, produces modest red, white and rosé wines.

Faugères and **St-Chinian** are still relatively unknown but none the less good-value appellations for red and rosé wines.

Minervois is predominantly red, from the hills to the east of Carcassonne. The wines tend to be full-bodied and rich.

Cabardes is a VDQS, north of Carcassonne, whose red wines, particularly those that include Cabernet and Merlot with the Midi varieties, are rightly becoming better known.

Corbières covers a large area to the south of Carcassonne and the best wines tend to come from the higher vineyards, notably the Côtes d'Alaric. Quality, particularly of the reds, has improved dramatically over the last ten years, with increased use of the better grape varieties, more careful vinification and the use of oak casks for ageing.

Fitou is one of the oldest appellations in the Languedoc and covers two small areas on the border with Roussillon. Only red wine is produced, from up to 75 per cent Carignan grapes, and it must be aged for 9 months in barrel. Its rich, supple flavour has made it among the most popular of the region's appellations.

There are several appellations for Vin Doux Naturel, made from the Muscat grape: **Lunel**, **Mireval**, **Frontignan**, **St-Jean de Minervois**, all similar in style to Beaumes de Venise.

The main appellations in Roussillon are:

Côtes du Roussillon, which covers a large area south of the Corbières. Red, white and rosé wines are all improving in quality; the red and rosé are predominantly from Carignan, the white from Macabeo.

Côtes du Roussillon Villages is an exclusively red wine appellation for 25 villages in the northern section, bordering Corbières. The wines tend to have more character than straight Côtes du Roussillon; the two best villages are

Caramany and Latour de France, which may include their name on the label.

Rivesaltes is the largest appellation for Vin Doux Naturel in France. The red wines, from Grenache, take on a tawny colour after being aged for a long time.

Muscat de Rivesaltes is another Vin Doux Naturel, made exclusively from Muscat grapes.

Banyuls is the most southerly appellation in France, right on the Spanish border. Its Vin Doux Naturel, primarily from Grenache, is certainly the finest in France; the best wines are entitled to label themselves Grand Cru.

Collioure is a full, dry red produced from the same grapes and in the same area as Banyuls.

Corsica produces red, white and rosé wines, the quality of which is improving, although most is still consumed locally.

THE LOIRE VALLEY

The Loire is the longest river in France; from its source in the Cévennes it flows for over 1000 km, first north to Nevers, then in a long curve westwards as far as Orleans, from where it heads due west to Nantes and the Atlantic. Over such a distance, there is obviously a great variety of wine styles; the four main wine regions, going eastwards from the Atlantic, are the area around Nantes, Anjou and Saumur, Touraine, and the Central Vineyards. The Loire

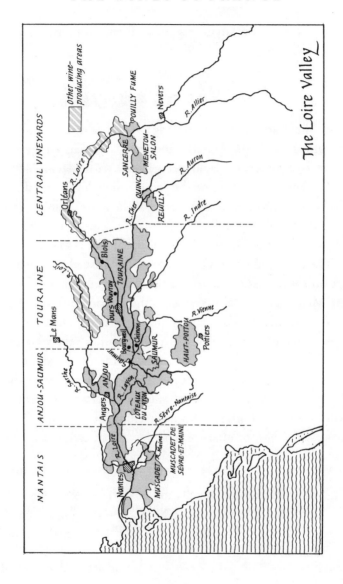

The Loire Valley

Valley is the third largest region in France for Appellation Contrôlée wines.

The Nantes district

The climate around Nantes is fairly wet and damp as a result of the proximity of the Atlantic, and while summers are warm, winters can be very cold and spring frosts a particular problem.

The best vineyards lie on the gently rolling hills around the rivers Sèvre and Maine, tributaries of the Loire. The soil is a mixture of sand, gravel and clay over a schistous, volcanic subsoil. Good drainage is essential in the wet climate.

The Nantes district is best known for **Muscadet**, which is grown south-east of the city. The wine takes its name from the Muscadet vine, also known as the Melon de Bourgogne or Gamay Blanc. This variety produces fairly bland wine, with a high natural acidity. Fruit and flavour in the wine are enhanced by leaving it in contact with the yeast sediments from fermentation until bottling. In order to qualify for the designation 'Sur Lie', the wine must stay on the lees over the winter and be bottled without racking or filtering. This process also has the effect of retaining a little carbonic gas in the wine which gives it extra bite and freshness.

The basic **Muscadet** appellation mainly covers vineyards on flat land really unsuitable for the production of good wine, and only accounts for 10 per cent of the total production.

Muscadet de Sèvre et Maine accounts for three-quarters of the production, although the appellation only covers a quarter of the vineyard area. Almost 50 per cent is bottled and sold 'Sur Lie'. The best wines are light, fresh and crisp, with good fruit and acidity. Muscadet is the only Appellation Contrôlée in France that has a maximum, rather than minimum, level of alcohol – 12 per cent – to ensure that the wines are not too heavy.

Muscadet des Coteaux de la Loire is a small area north-east of Nantes, producing wines even higher in acidity.

Coteaux d'Ancenis is a VDQS for varietal wines from Cabernet, Gamay, Chenin Blanc and Malvoisie, grown in the same area as Muscadet des Coteaux de la Loire.

Gros Plant is the local name for the Folle Blanche grape, and is a VDQS which is even lighter and more acidic than Muscadet, although it does have a local following.

Anjou and Saumur

The region of Anjou/Saumur is a microcosm of the Loire in general, producing a whole variety of different wines, red, white and rosé, dry and sweet, still and sparkling. Whilst still best known for the ubiquitous Anjou Rosé, which accounts for around 50 per cent of the area's production, the best wines from the region are the reds and sparkling whites.

The region benefits from a slightly drier climate than the

Nantes district to the west, although the Atlantic is still an important influence. There is a wide variety of microclimates which explains the large diversity of wines produced in the region.

The characteristic soil is the chalk tufa around Saumur, which provided the stone used for building many of the châteaux of the Loire, including that of Saumur itself. The excavation of the stone created cellars ideal for storing wine.

The most important grape varieties are Chenin Blanc (sometimes called the Pineau de la Loire) for the white wines and Cabernet-Franc, Gamay (known locally as Cot) and Grolleau for the red and rosé wines.

Anjou

Anjou is the largest appellation as growers in Saumur may also use the name instead of their own. Whilst the soft, medium-sweet rosé wines are the best known, it is the reds from Cabernet-Franc which are the most interesting.

Cabernet d'Anjou is an appellation reserved solely for rosé wines made from the Cabernet as opposed to the Grolleau, which is the dominant variety in straight Anjou Rosé.

Savennières is a small area, south-west of Angers, which produces the best dry white wines of the region using the Chemin Blanc grape. The secret is a particular outcrop of blue volcanic rock brought downriver from the Massif Central and now embedded in the vineyard soil.

Coteaux du Layon produces excellent sweet white wine

from the Chenin Blanc, grown on stony, schistous soil along the river Layon, a tributary of the Loire. The steep, south-facing slopes give protection from the prevailing winds, and the resulting microclimate means that the grapes are some-times attacked by noble rot. Even in years without botrytis, the best vineyards are harvested several times in *tries* (successive pickings of the affected grape). The yields are restricted to 30 hectolitres per hectare and the wine must reach a minimum 13 per cent alcohol, much the same as Sauternes. The main difference between the two is the extra acidity from the Chenin grape, allied to the cooler climate, which makes the wines from Coteaux du Layon particularly long-lived.

Coteaux du Layon Villages is reserved for 6 villages considered to produce higher-quality wine. **Coteaux du Layon Chaume** has a lower maximum yield of 25 hecto-litres per hectare and is thus richer and more concentrated.

Quarts de Chaume comprises only 100 acres on a plateau above the village of Chaume; its wines are a little lighter and higher in acidity than those of Bonnezeaux, and these two vineyards are considered the finest in the area for sweet wine.

Bonnezeaux has a particularly good southerly exposure for its 300 acres in the commune of Thouarce. Its sweet, honeyed wines are generally a little fuller than Quarts de Chaume, with a minimum sugar content even higher than that required for Sauternes.

Saumur

Saumur is best known for its sparkling wines, although the appellation also covers still white and red. The sparkling wine industry of Saumur is second only to that of Champagne in France, and the wines have to be bottle-fermented. They can be produced from red and white grapes, as in Champagne, although here it is the Chenin Blanc and Cabernet-Franc which are the principal varieties; up to 20 per cent Chardonnay is also allowed. The wines have the high natural acidity required for making sparkling wine, thanks to the Chenin Blanc grape, and the chalk/tufa soil of the region provides perfect ageing cellars.

Crémant de Loire is another appellation that may be used for sparkling wines made by bottle-fermentation, but which are less fizzy, with a pressure of 3.5 rather than 5–6 atmospheres.

Of the still wines of Saumur, the reds from Cabernet-Franc are generally better than the whites, as the Chenin Blanc tends to produce light, rather tart, appley wines, except in hot summers.

Saumur-Champigny is a small area to the east of Saumur which produces the best red wines of the area. Made from Cabernet Franc with a little Cabernet-Sauvignon, these wines generally have a rich, sweet fruit flavour.

Many of these red wines from the Loire are served cool, or even chilled, particularly in France. Whilst they are often light and fruity, in hot years they can be quite full and tannic and should therefore be treated in the same manner as the wines of Bordeaux.

Touraine

Touraine is often referred to as the Garden of France; in fact the Vin de Pays denomination that covers the whole of the Loire Valley is Vin de Pays du Jardin de la France. The region enjoys a mild, temperate climate, with greater protection from the Atlantic, which is beneficial to the cultivation of a wide variety of fruit and vegetables.

The area around Tours has the same chalk/tufa found in Saumur, but there is a more clayey soil, mixed with sand or gravel, in the west of the region, and it is here that the best red wines of the Loire are produced.

The principal grape varieties are Cabernet-Franc (known locally as Breton) and Gamay for the red wines, and Chenin and Sauvignon Blanc for the white.

The appellation **Touraine** covers the whole region and produces a wide range of wines, the best being single varietal wines, particularly Sauvignon, Gamay and Cabernet-Franc. The best white wines can be a useful, cheaper alternative to Sancerre. Azay-le-Rideau, Amboise and Mesland are three small areas which may add their name to the appellation Touraine.

Bourgueil is made from Cabernet-Franc grown mostly on a sandy, gravelly soil on the north bank of the Loire, east of Saumur; some of the vineyards lying further away from the river are on a more chalk/clay plateau and are generally considered to produce finer wine. Up to 10 per cent Cabernet-Sauvignon may be added to Cabernet-Franc and the best wines from the hottest summers repay keeping.

St-Nicolas-de-Bourgueil has its own appellation due to a more sandy soil which generally produces somewhat lighter wines. Both Bourgueil and St-Nicolas produce small amounts of rosé wine.

Chinon lies south of the Loire, with its vineyards either side of the river Vienne. Made from Cabernet-Franc grown on a chalk/clay soil, the reds tend to be a little lighter than Bourgueil, although again the best are still quite rich and will benefit from maturation in bottle. Chinon also produces rosé and white; the latter from Chenin Blanc can be very good.

Vouvray is the best-known white wine from Touraine. Made from the Chenin Blanc, it can be dry, *demi-sec* or sweet; still, *pétillant* or fully sparkling. The vineyards lie to the east of Tours on a chalk/clay soil and in sunny years the grapes can be affected by noble rot and make rich, honeyed sweet wines. Otherwise they tend to be quite hard and acidic, but provide good base wine to be made sparkling using the bottle-fermentation method.

Montlouis lies opposite Vouvray, on the south bank of the Loire, and although it is a less well-known appellation it makes a similar range and style of wine from the Chenin Blanc.

Coteaux du Loir is an appellation for red, white and rosé wines produced north of Tours, along the river Loir, a tributary of the Loire.

Jasnières is small appellation within the Coteaux du Loir producing very good white wine from Chenin Blanc.

Cheverny is a VDQS area south of Blois at the eastern end of the region, producing good-quality, mostly varietal, red, white and rosé wines.

Haut-Poitou is another VDQS, 180 km south-west of Tours, which has achieved great success, mainly due to the local co-operative, with its varietal wines, particularly Sauvignon, Cabernet and Gamay.

The Central Vineyards

Central Vineyards is a convenient term under which to group the collection of appellations, south-east of Orleans, which lie roughly in the centre of France. Being the most easterly of the Loire vineyards, they have a more continental climate with hotter summers and colder winters; spring frosts are a perennial hazard.

The vineyards lie on chalk hillsides, with a mixture of clay and flint in the soil. Sauvignon Blanc is the dominant grape variety.

Sancerre's vineyards lie on the west bank of the Loire. Sancerre is best known for its white wine, but prior to the devastation of the vineyards by phylloxera in the last century, the red wines made from Pinot Noir were more important. These are now increasing in popularity again; in sunny years they can compare with a light red Burgundy. Rosé Sancerre is also produced.

White Sancerre should have the tart, grassy, gooseberry fruit flavour of the Sauvignon grape, although there are considerable variations in style among the different growers of the 14 communes within the appellation.

Pouilly-Fumé is equally well known – its wines should not be confused with Pouilly-Fuisse in Burgundy. The vineyards lie on the east bank of the Loire, opposite those of Sancerre, and the wines are generally lighter with more finesse, often with a smokiness on the palate. The wines can be labelled as Pouilly-Blanc-Fumé or Blanc-Fumé de Pouilly.

Pouilly-sur-Loire is an appellation for wines made not from the classic Sauvignon but from Chasselas, better known as a table grape.

Reuilly, though less well-known than Sancerre or Pouilly, produces good-quality whites from Sauvignon, as well as red and rosé from Pinot.

Quincy, like Reuilly, lies in the crook of the Loire, west of the town of Bourges, but is exclusively white, from Sauvignon.

Menetou-Salon, north of Bourges, produces very good

white from Sauvignon Blanc and red and rosé wines from Pinot Noir. These last three appellations can often offer better value than their better-known neighbours of Sancerre and Pouilly.

ALSACE

The wine-producing region of Alsace lies in the very north-east of France, bordering Switzerland to the south and Germany to the east, across the river Rhine. It is an area that has suffered more than most at the hands of history. Having been ceded to France by the Treaty of Westphalia in 1648, which ended the Thirty Years War, it came under German control in 1871 at the end of the Franco-Prussian War, and remained so until the end of the First World War and the Treaty of Versailles. The region witnessed extensive fighting during the Second World War, when it was reclaimed by Germany in 1940 and only returned to France after the Liberation.

Alsace was at one time regarded simply as a source of bulk table wine by the Germans, but after the war, growers aimed for quality. The plantings of mainly Chasselas and Sylvaner on the fertile valley floor were uprooted and replaced by better varieties planted on the hillsides. Appellation Contrôlée status for the region was only achieved in 1962, and then the appellation accorded was simply **Vin d'Alsace**, which covers all the wines, 95 per cent of which are sold as single-grape varieties. In 1975 the appellation Alsace Grand

Cru was introduced, but it was not until 1983 that the first list of 25 Grand Cru sites was published. A further 23 were added three years later. The Grand Cru appellation can only be applied to wines made from four grape varieties grown in the specified sites of Riesling, Gewürztraminer, Muscat and Tokay-Pinot Gris.

Alsace is the most northerly vineyard area in France with the exception of Champagne, yet it enjoys a semi-continental climate. Protected on the west by the Vosges mountains, the vineyards lie on the sheltered eastern slopes mostly facing south or south-east. Colmar, at the centre of the wine-growing area, is the second driest town in France, with an average annual rainfall of about 480 mm, almost half the average 850 mm in Bordeaux.

The Vosges mountains give better protection to the vineyards of the Haut-Rhin in the south of the region, where they rise to 1400 m, compared to the Bas-Rhin in the north, where they reach a height of only 600 m. The best vineyards are generally found in the middle of the slopes at an altitude of between 150 and 400 m, with protection afforded by the forests on the tops of the hills.

The soil in Alsace is very varied and determines the grape variety grown on each site. It is often quite a rich loam, mixed with limestone, granite or sand, with a more alluvial soil at the bottom of the hills. Generally the soil is heavier in the northern Bas-Rhin, favouring the growing of Sylvaner and Auxerrois rather than the noble varieties.

The vines are trained high to reduce the danger from

spring frosts, and to reduce some of the influence of the rich soil, as well as to maximize exposure to the sun.

Nearly all Alsace wines are fully fermented dry, with the exception of those which are late-harvested and contain a certain degree of residual sugar. These wines are labelled Vendange Tardive or Sélection de Grains Nobles, and they can only be made from grapes with a stipulated minimum sugar content. Sélection de Grains Nobles can only really be produced from grapes which have been affected to a certain degree by noble rot.

All Alsace wine must be bottled within the two departments of Haut-Rhin and Bas-Rhin, in the traditional green fluted bottle.

Main grape varieties

Edelzwicker is not actually a grape variety but an appellation for a blend of different varieties. Normally these wines are predominantly Sylvaner or Pinot Blanc, and provide light, fruity, easy-drinking wines which are a good introduction to Alsace.

Sylvaner is the most widely planted variety in Alsace and, being high-yielding, generally produces rather bland, earthy wines, but the best examples do show some spicy fruit flavour.

Pinot Blanc (also known locally as Klevner) again mostly produces light, bland wine, but many which are so labelled contain a good proportion of Auxerrois, which can give more body. Those actually labelled as Auxerrois are rarely seen, but this variety is widely grown in the Bas-Rhin.

Pinot Noir produces a very pale, light red in the northerly climate of Alsace. These wines often make up for lack of body with a soft and fragrant, raspberry fruit flavour.

Tokay-Pinot Gris is so called to distinguish it from Tokay in Hungary, to which it bears no resemblance. In Alsace it produces rich, quite full-bodied, spicy wines.

Muscat produces its best wines in Alsace in summers without too much heat, so its natural acidity can balance the flowery, aromatic, grapey flavours. These are among the few dry Muscat wines produced anywhere.

Gewürztraminer is the variety which most expresses the Alsatian wine style – smelling sweet but tasting dry. Gewürztraminer has a very distinctive, dried rose-petal aroma, but a full-bodied, rich and concentrated flavour. Those which contain residual sugar from late-picked grapes are among the most voluptuous of wines.

Riesling is again nearly always dry in Alsace. It can have a hard, steely edge, particularly in light years when the grape's natural acidity can make the wine taste very austere. But in hotter years, and with age, these wines can achieve wonderful depths of flavour.

CHAMPAGNE

The word champagne has come to symbolize the ultimate quality lifestyle. But the name has been hijacked world-wide not only by producers of sparkling wine, but also of other fruit drinks and even perfume. **Champagne** is actually an appellation for wines produced from specified grape varieties grown in a delimited region of northern France, which have undergone a second fermentation in the bottle. Within the EC, the term champagne is restricted to these wines; however, sparkling wines produced and sold elsewhere still use the name to increase the credibility of their product.

Legend has it that champagne, as a sparkling wine, was invented by Dom Pérignon, monk and cellar-master at the Abbey of Hautvillers at the end of the seventeenth century. However, it is clear that the wine of the region was already being sold as a sparkling wine – most likely as a simple result of being bottled prior to having undergone its malolactic fermentation, which then occurred in the bottle, creating a certain effervescence.

Dom Perignon was one of several important figures responsible over the years for the development of the sparkling wine we know today. He introduced the idea of blending different grape varieties from different villages within the region to produce a more harmonious wine, and of using a shallow, vertical press to avoid colour from the use of black grapes. He also sought to develop stronger glass and the use of corks to retain the sparkle in the bottle.

The process of creating a secondary fermentation in the bottle developed over two centuries, and became known as the *méthode champenoise*. The EC is now prohibiting the use of this term by producers of sparkling wines outside the Champagne region.

Champagne is the most northerly of all Appellation Contrôlée regions in France, lying 180 km north-east of Paris. The cool climate – Champagne is almost at the limit for successful cultivation of the vine – means that the grapes have a long growing cycle. The danger from late spring frosts is a very real one, although the continental summers mean that there is usually sufficient sunshine to ripen the grapes. However, the natural alcohol levels are low and acidity high.

The soil structure in Champagne provides the key to the unique quality which the best wines can achieve. The subsoil is part of a sea-bed which dried up 69 million years ago. Subsequent earthquakes, the last 11 million years ago, created the hills of the Champagne region and at the same time threw up tertiary deposits, particularly lignite, which formed a rich topsoil. The height of the vineyards, up to 200 m above sea-level, helps to compensate for the northerly climate.

The only grapes allowed in the production of champagne are Chardonnay, Pinot Noir and Pinot Meunier. Chardonnay is very resistant to low temperatures and produces better wine from low yields, so is ideally suited to champagne. It produces wines with body and richness, well balanced in

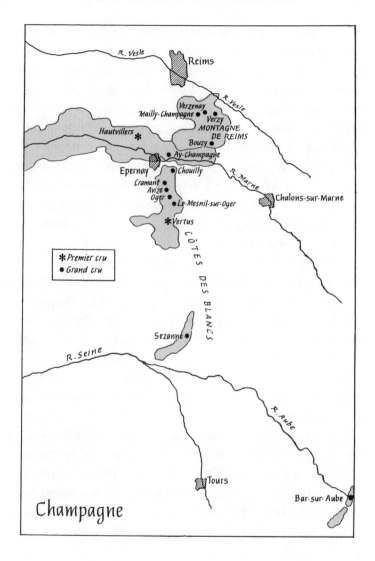

Reims

R. Vesle

R. Vesle

Verzenay
Mailly-Champagne
Verzy
MONTAGNE
DE REIMS
Bouzy
Hautvillers *
Ay-Champagne
Epernay
R. Marne
Chouilly
Cramant
Avize
Oger
Le-Mesnil-sur-Oger
Chalons-sur-Marne
*Vertus

* Premier cru
• Grand cru

CÔTES DES BLANCS

Sezanne •

R. Seine

R. Aube

Tours

Bar-sur-Aube •

Champagne

alcohol and acidity, and gives elegance and finesse to the blend. Most of the Chardonnay in Champagne is grown on the Côte des Blancs, the range of hills running south from Epernay, and further south on the Côte de Sézanne. The Pinot Noir likes a long, gradual growing season and gives body, structure and backbone to the wine. It is mostly cultivated on the Montagne de Reims, between Reims and Epernay, and in the Aube vineyards in the south of the region. Pinot Meunier is a variant of Pinot Noir which is more resistant to frosts and better suited to the sandier soils along the valley of the Marne. Its coarser style means that it is used in higher proportions in lower-quality blends.

Five distinct districts make up the Champagne region. The vineyards are classified on a scale of between 80 and 100 per cent, which determines the price paid for the grapes by the champagne houses or co-operatives. There are 17 villages which are classified 100 per cent, known as Grands Crus, and are considered to produce the finest wines. Forty villages are classified between 90 and 99 per cent, and are known as Premiers Crus. The Grands and Premiers Crus represent about a third of the total vineyard area of Champagne. All the Grand and Premier Cru villages are in the three major districts of the Montagne de Reims, Vallée de la Marne and Côte des Blancs. The two outlying districts in the south, the Côte de Sézanne and the Aube, can only aspire to 80 per cent classification, but this has never prevented the major champagne houses buying their grapes.

The champagne industry is made up very distinctly of growers and the major champagne firms. There are approximately 14,000 growers in the Champagne region, of whom no more than 5000 make wine themselves. The majority sell all their grapes to the champagne houses or co-operatives. There are around 120 champagne houses, although 50 per cent of sales of champagne are made by the 10 largest firms. Twenty-eight firms belong to the Syndicat des Grandes Marques de Champagne, which although including the top names also encompasses some very mediocre brands. The champagne houses own only around 15 per cent of the vineyards, so are required to buy in grapes from the growers. The price paid for the grapes every year is determined by the percentage rating of the village against a reference price established prior to the vintage, by a committee of growers and producers. At a guideline price of FF25.00 per kilo, a grower in an 80 per cent village would receive only FF20.00 whilst a grower in a 100 per cent village would receive the full FF25.00. The best champagne houses will have an average above 90 per cent in their standard non-vintage blends.

Harvesting in Champagne must be carried out by hand; mechanical harvesting would damage the grapes too severely and lead to coloration of the must prior to fermentation. For the same reason, the grapes also have to be sorted to remove any that are damaged. The pressing must be carried out quickly, particularly with Pinot, Noir and Meunier to avoid colouring the juice. For this reason the major firms have presses throughout the region, and there are nearly 150 co-operatives. The grapes are still mainly pressed in the traditional vertical presses. These hold 4000 kilos of grapes, from which only 2550 litres of wine may be pressed; the first pressing produces 2050 litres and is called the *vin de cuvée*, which represents the best must; the second pressing produces 500 litres of *vin de taille*, which will be coarser and will not be used in the very best blends, but sold to producers of cheaper brands.

Once the wines have undergone a normal alcoholic fermentation, the all-important task of the *assemblage*, or blending, begins. Most champagne sold is non-vintage, so the blending will be not only with different wines from different districts, but also with reserve wine from earlier vintages, so as to keep the style of a particular brand consistent.

The méthode champenoise

Addition of the liqueur de tirage

Prior to bottling, a mixture of reserve wine, sugar and selected yeasts is added to the still wine. The wine is filled into the bottles in which it will eventually be sold. It is sealed with a crown cap over a small plastic cup which in due course will collect the spent yeast cells. The wines are then stored on their sides in cellars, many of which date from Roman times when they were excavated for building materials.

Prise de mousse

The yeasts immediately start converting the sugars to alcohol and carbon dioxide gas, but in the cool cellars this second fermentation can last up to three months. As there is nowhere for this gas to escape, it becomes absorbed in the wine, creating the sparkle.

The wines are aged lying on their sides. Non-vintage champagne cannot be sold until one year from the January following the vintage. The better wines will be aged for longer, as yeast autolysis will occur. This is the gradual breakdown of the dead yeast cells which will give the champagne its unique flavour. Vintage champagne must be aged for at least three years, and again the best wines will be aged longer.

However, the sediment created by the spent yeast cells has to be removed.

Remuage

The traditional method for removing the sediment was developed by Madame Clicquot, a widow who gave her name to the famous house of Veuve Clicquot. The bottles are placed neck-up in rectangular boards, hinged at the top, with 60 holes. Starting from the horizontal position in which they lay during the second fermentation, they are shaken, twisted and raised by hand, every day for two months, up to a vertical position, neck down. This has the effect of forcing the sediment into the neck of the bottle. Many firms are now using gyropallets which hold 500 bottles in a wire cage and are computer-controlled to rotate round on two axes, to create the same effect. The bottles are subsequently kept *sur pointes*, neck-down, until the point of disgorging.

Dégorgement

This is the removal of the yeast sediment in the neck of the bottle. Today, this is nearly always done by passing the bottle necks through brine, which freezes the sediment in the plastic cup in the neck. The bottle can then be turned upright, the crown cap removed, and the pressure from the carbonic gas in the bottle will force out the cup of frozen sediment with very little loss of wine. The bottles are then refilled and sealed on rotating fillers as quickly as possible, so as not to lose pressure.

Addition of liqueur d'expédition

The bottles are not topped up solely with the same wine, but with a mixture of reserve wine and sugar, known as *dosage*. The naturally high acidity, especially in young champagne, necessitates a little softening, and even the driest style of champagne usually has a small *dosage*. The bottles are immediately corked and secured with a wire muzzle. The wine will then normally be given time to rest before being sold; it is often considered worth cellaring it for a further one or two years.

Main champagne styles

Non-vintage 75 per cent of champagne sales are of non-vintage, and the reputation of a champagne house will normally rest on the quality and consistency of their blend. Most of these wines are sold as Brut or Extra-Dry – these wines will have had very little sugar added in the form of *dosage*. A champagne labelled 'Sec' will in fact be a little less dry, and one labelled 'Demi-Sec' will more likely be medium-sweet. A small amount of champagne is sold as 'Doux', or rich, and can be a wonderful accompaniment to puddings.

Vintage champagne is normally only produced in those years when the climatic conditions produce a well-balanced wine. Because these years will produce the best wines, and as they have to be aged for a minimum of three years before sale, they will always be more expensive than the non-vintage equivalent from the same house.

Blanc de Blancs champagne is made exclusively from Chardonnay grapes, and is therefore most likely to originate from the Côte des Blancs. Given age, Blanc de Blanc champagne will exhibit the rich, toasted flavour of Chardonnay.

Blanc de Noirs will be made exclusively from Pinot Noir or Pinot Meunier grapes, but is rarely labelled as such. Many individual producers' champagnes from those areas growing predominantly these varieties will in fact be Blanc de Noirs although there will be no indication of this.

Rosé champagne is normally produced by the addition of a small amount of still red wine to the sparkling white. In fact it is the only Appellation Contrôlée wine in France where this is allowed. A few firms do, however, make rosé champagne with skin contact, although this appears not to make a discernible difference to the final taste.

Crémant is a style that has less pressure than traditional champagne – 3.5 atmospheres rather than 5–6 – and this gives the wine a softer, creamier quality.

Coteaux Champenois is the appellation reserved for the still red and white wines produced in the Champagne region. These wines are generally light, thin and high in acidity and are nearly always over-priced.

Rosé des Riceys is a still, pink wine produced in very small quantities in the village of the same name in the Aube.

The price of a bottle of champagne to the consumer can vary significantly. As has been noted above, the source of the grapes, the use of first or second pressing, the length of maturation will all have a significant effect on the cost. The advertising and promotional budgets, as well as sales policy, of the major firms will also influence the price paid by the consumer. There is, however, a vast difference between a champagne produced from the second pressings of 80 percent-rated villages sold after only one year and the prestige *cuvées* made by the leading champagne houses.

Unfortunately the champagne label does not give much information to the consumer. A growers' label may show whether the wine is Grand or Premier Cru, but there is no indication as to whether it was made exclusively from the *cuvée*, or of the length of ageing. The only clue can be the matriculation number at the bottom of the label, which every producer in Champagne must show, preceded by his status.

NM stands for *négociant-manipulant*, a firm which buys in grapes; every major champagne house buys in at least 5 per cent of its requirement, many as much as 95 percent.

RM is a *récoltant-manipulant*, a grower who produces his own champagne.

CM is the product of a *co-operative-manipulant*.

MA is a *marque-auxilière* a brand-name owned by the producer or purchaser.

The last two are most likely to be seen on supermarket or house brands, often referred to as **BOB** (buyer's own brand) champagne.

Champagne is normally considered an apéritif or a drink for receptions. However, with its variety of styles, it can also accompany a meal right the way through.

Sparkling Wines

The champagne method of secondary fermentation in the bottle is widely used for producing sparkling wines through-out the world. However, the term 'méthode champenoise' is no longer allowed to be shown on the bottle to indicate this fact, and the use of 'méthode traditionelle' is replacing it.

There is a much cheaper method of producing sparkling wine which is to create the second fermentation in large sealed tanks – known as the 'cuve close' system. The sparkling wine is then filtered from the tanks straight into the bottle, thus avoiding the time and expense of remuage and disgorging. Although this method is normally used for cheaper sparkling wines, it should be remembered that the quality of any sparkling wine is as much dependent on the quality of the base wine and the length of time the wine spends on the yeasts as the method of production.

CHAPTER FOUR

THE WINES OF GERMANY

Germany, despite having only 1 per cent of the world's vineyard area, produces 13 per cent of its wines. The country lies at the climatic limit for wine production, and the essence of German wines is the balance of grape sugars with high natural acidity. The classification of Germany's quality wines is based on the natural sugar levels in the grapes at the time of harvest; although these sugars can be fully fermented out, the majority of German wines retain their natural sweetness to a greater or lesser degree.

A very small proportion of German wine is not classified as quality wine; only if the natural must weight of the grapes fails to reach a specific gravity of 1050, giving a potential alcohol level of just 6 per cent, will the wine be graded as Deutscher Tafelwein. A wine with a specific gravity of 1050 is described as having 50° Oechsle.

There are 13 specified wine-producing regions in Germany, called **Anbaugebiete**, where **Qualitätswein** is produced. These wines are often abbreviated to **ObA, Qualitätswein bestimmter Anbaugebiete**. Except in unusually hot years, the majority of wine produced each year in Germany is at the Qualitätswein level.

Within the 13 Anbaugebiete there are 38 wine districts,

or **Bereiche**, which contain a total of 152 collective, as opposed to individual, vineyard sites, called **Grosslagen**. These cover a very large area.

There are a further 2635 individual vineyards, **Einzella-gen**, a number severely reduced from 25,000 vineyard names by the 1971 German Wine Law. Unfortunately for the consumer, there is no indication on the label of German wine as to whether it comes from a Grosslage, which is at best a modest, generic wine, or an Einzellage, in which case it should have some real individual character of the site where it was grown.

Wines made from grapes with a higher natural sugar content than that required for Qualitätswein will qualify for the superior grade of **Qualitätswein mit Prädikat (QmP)**. The yields for QmP wines produced in the five Rhine regions are more restricted than for QbA and wines cannot be chaptalized to increase their alcoholic degree. A QmP wine can only be the produce of one Bereich. There are 6 predicates, in ascending order of sweeetness:

Kabinett denotes wines which have a higher degree Oechsle than is required for Qualitätswein. These will be fuller, rather than sweeter, wines.

Spätlese is made from grapes harvested at least 7 days later than the main harvest. These will generally be sweeter.

Auslese is made from selected bunches of grapes which have been left even longer on the vine. These wines will usually be quite sweet.

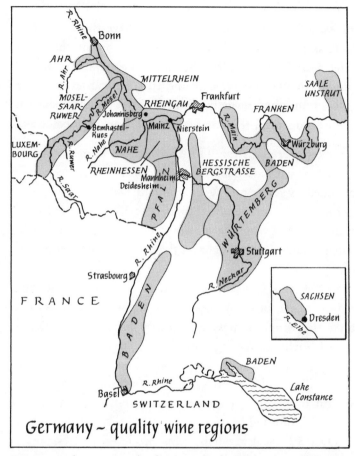

Germany ~ quality wine regions

Beerenauslese is made from individually selected berries which have been affected by *Edelfaule* (noble rot). Although the minimum Oechsle level required would give a potential alcohol of over 15 per cent, the laws require only 5.5 per cent, so these wines have a high level of residual sugar.

Eiswein is made from grapes which have the same sugar level as required for Beerenauslese, but are only harvested after becoming frozen on the vine. The grapes are quickly pressed in their frozen state and thus have an even greater concentration of sugar. Due to the difficulties involved in their production, these wines are both rare and expensive.

Trockenbeerenauslese (TBA) is made from individual berries which have been left to dry on the vine after being attacked by noble rot. With a potential strength of over 20 per cent, but only required to achieve 5.5 per cent alcohol, these very rare wines have a deep amber colour and such an intense, concentrated richness that they can only be sipped.

All QbA and QmP wines have to show their Amtliche Prufnummer, or AP number, on the label. This is awarded after the wine has passed a quality control examination, which includes testing for ripeness in the vineyard at harvest, analysis to measure alcohol, residual sugar, extract and acidity, and a 'blind' tasting to confirm that the wine is typical of the origin, grape variety, quality category and vintage submitted.

Over 80 per cent of the wine produced in Germany is white. The majority of wines indicate the grape variety on the label, which actually means that the wine is made with a minimum of 85 per cent of that variety.

Müller-Thurgau is the most widely planted grape variety in Germany. It is a crossing developed in 1882 by a Professor

Müller from Thurgau in Switzerland, and has been successful because it ripens early and can produce a large yield. It has a soft, grapey aroma, with less acidity than Riesling, and is responsible for a large proportion of Liebfraumilch and similar-style wines, particularly from the Rheinhessen and Rheinpfalz.

Riesling produces nearly all the classic and best wines in Germany, but, because it is a late ripener and produces low yields, it is usually only planted in the best vineyard sites. It grows well in poor soil, particularly the slate of the Mosel, but its thin skin makes it susceptible to botrytis. From the best sites on the Mosel and the Rheingau the Riesling produces wines which are crisp and steely with good acidity when young but take on a more honeyed, petrolly character with age.

Silvaner ripens earlier than Riesling, but does not produce wines with the same attack; they tend to be softer and fairly neutral. The best come from Franconia.

There are many plantings of various crossings, particularly Kerner, Scheurebe and Bacchus, but these rarely come close to matching the Riesling for quality.

Germany's red wines are made primarily from the Spätburgunder (Pinot Noir), or Portugieser.

The majority of German wines are fully fermented out; that is, all the grape sugars are converted to alcohol. Many of the wines at Qualitätswein level have a potential alcohol level of only 6 per cent, and this has to be augmented by chaptalization, the addition of sugar prior to fermentation. Even with all sugars fermented out the finished wines will have an alcoholic strength of only between 8 and 10 per cent. In order to give sweetness to balance the high acidity and natural austerity of these wines, *Süss-reserve* is added before bottling.

Süss-reserve is unfermented grape juice which should be of the same origin and quality level as the wine to which it will be added. The grape juice has been sterilized by removing the yeasts and is added in proportion to the alcohol level of the wine. It is *Süss-reserve* which gives German wines their sweet, grapey character and helps to balance the acidity.

Many of the best German wines, particularly of QmP quality, will be fermented more carefully to retain a level of sweetness without having to resort to the later addition of *Süss-reserve*. Chaptalization, to increase the alcohol level, is not allowed for QmP wines.

There has been an increase in the production of wines with lower levels of residual sugar, which have achieved sales success in Germany, although not, it has to be said, in the export market. Wines labelled **Trocken** (dry) must not contain more than 9 grams per litre of residual sugar; **Halbtrocken** (medium-dry) wines may not contain more than 18 grams per litre of residual sugar. In order to have sufficient body, such wines really need to be of at least Spätlese quality.

There is a very important sparkling wine industry in Germany, mainly for home consumption. The vast majority is sold simply as **Sekt** and is made from imported wine, usually from France or Italy, with the second fermentation taking place in pressurized tanks (the *cuve close* method). Sparkling wines labelled as **Deutscher Sekt** must be made only from grapes grown in Germany; the best wines will be made from Riesling and will exhibit its grapey character. **Deutscher Sekt bA**, or **Deutscher Qualitätsschaumwein bA**, is a sparkling wine from one specific Anbaugebiete.

The most important wine-producing regions in Germany are:

Mosel-Saar-Ruwer

The vineyards of the Mosel follow the river northwards to Koblenz from the French border, south of Trier, where the Ruwer and Saar tributaries flow into it. The best vineyards are on the steep slopes along the Mosel, which, with the river's many twists and turns, provide the ideal aspect for maximum exposure to the sun. The best vineyards in the Middle Mosel have a slate soil, rich in minerals, whilst there is more limestone in the Saar and Ruwer valleys. The river valleys help to temper the generally cool climate, and afford protection to the vines, whilst the slate soil increases the effects of the sun by reflection. The Mosel is ideally suited to the Riesling grape.

There are 5 Bereiche in the Mosel-Saar-Ruwer, the best-known of which is **Bereich Bernkastel**. Of the 192 communes whose names may appear on the label, the best-known in the Middle Mosel, with their best Einzellage in brackets, are **Piesport** (Goldtropfchen), **Brauneberg** (Juffer), **Bernkastel** (Doktor), **Graach** (Himmelreich), **Wehlen** (Sonnenuhr) and **Urzig** (Wurzgarten). Of the 20 Grosslagen in the Mosel, **Piesporter Michelsberg** is the best known ('er' is added to the village name when it is followed by a vineyard name), although its wines are generally very modest, coming from predominantly Müller-Thurgau grapes grown on the flat plains away from the river slopes. Much better quality wine is found in the Grosslagen of **Badstübe** and **Kurfürstlay** in Bernkastel.

The primary characteristic of Mosel wines is their racy acidity, balanced by a soft, sweet grapeyness. Even in hot years, the sweeter styles will still have a crisp bite to them, often enhanced by a little carbonic gas in the wine. These are very much wines to drink on their own, although they could accompany light fish dishes, or cold meats and salads in the summer.

Mosel wines are nearly always bottled in green glass, whereas the traditional brown hock bottle is used for wines from the Rhine.

Rheingau

The Rheingau is a very small region on the north bank of the Rhine as it flows westwards from Mainz to Bingen. The vineyards lie on south-facing slopes, well protected by the Taunus mountains to the north. The soil is a mixture of weathered slate mixed with loam and loess. The **Riesling** is again the dominant grape variety, accounting for over 80 per cent of the vineyards, although the blue-slate soil at Assmannshausen, in the extreme west of the region, favours the Spätburgunder, producing one of Germany's best red wines.

The Rheingau is home to many of the oldest and finest wine estates in Germany. It was here that the advantages of late picking and *Botrytis cinerea* were recognized. Today many of the leading procedures have formed an association of Charta estates to promote the drier styles of wine produced exclusively from the Riesling grape.

There is one Bereich in the region, **Johannisberg**, and 10 Grosslagen, of which the best-known is **Johannisberger Erntebringer**. (The Riesling grape grown elsewhere in the world is often called the Johannisberg Riesling to distinguish it from inferior variants.) All the villages – **Rudesheim**, **Geisenheim**, **Johannisberg**, **Winkel**, **Oestrich**, **Hattenheim**, **Erbach**, **Kiedrich**, **Rauenthal** and **Hochheim** – produce excellent wine. It is from the village of Hochheim, whose wines were a favourite with Queen Victoria, that the English word hock derived. This is now simply a generic term for any white wine from the Rhine.

The Rieslings from the Rheingau are generally fuller, with a more rounded, softer but spicier flavour, than those from the Mosel. It is this fullness which makes many of these wines better accompaniments to food, and certainly one of the aims of the Charta estates is to promote the drier styles as food wines. They can certainly match light spicy dishes of seafood, chicken and vegetables and go well with much oriental cuisine.

Rheinhessen

The vineyards of Rheinhessen cover a larger area than any other region of Germany. Unfortunately, much of the wine produced becomes the ubiquituous **Liebfraumilch**, 50 per cent of which is produced in the Rheinhessen. The origin of Liebfraumilch is in the wine produced from the vineyard of the Liebfrauenkirche, Church of Our Lady, in Worms. Today, however, Liebfraumilch can come from one of four different Anbaugebiete – Nahe, Rheingau, Rheinhessen and Rheinpfalz, although the last two account for 90 per cent. Despite this, Liebfraumilch was given Qualitätswein status in the 1971 German Wine Law, with specific regulations in respect of taste and sweetness. At best, it is a soft, light, medium-sweet white wine; at worst, and all too often, simply sugar-water.

The region is one of gently rolling hills to the south of Mainz, in the crook of the Rhein. The climate is temperate as it still benefits from the protection afforded by the Taunus mountains to the north. There is a variety of different soils, limestone, loess and sand, and of different grape varieties grown, particularly Müller-Thurgau and Silvaner. The best vineyards are found on the marlstone soil slopes facing the river, known as the Rhein Terrasse. It is here that the Riesling produces wines that are as far removed from Liebfraumilch as possible. The villages of **Nierstein** and **Oppenheim** contain some excellent Einzellagen, but unfortunately it is the inferior Grosslage of **Niersteiner Gutes Domtal** and **Bereich Nierstein** which are far better known.

Rheinpfalz

The Rheinpfalz, sometimes referred to as the Palatinate, lies to the south of the Rheinhessen and borders France to the south and west. It is the warmest region and produces the largest quantity of wine in Germany. The vineyards lie on gentle slopes along the eastern edge of the Haardt mountains, set back from the river Rhine. The soils are a mixture of sandstone, limestone and loam. The best sites are planted in Riesling, particularly in the villages of **Wachenheim**, **Forst** and **Deidesheim**, but again here large amounts of indifferent wine are produced from Müller-Thurgau, which helps to satisfy the export demand for Liebfraumilch.

Nahe

The Nahe, a tributary flowing into the Rhine at Bingen, is a region lying to the east of the Rheinhessen. Müller-Thurgau is the primary grape variety, but the best Einzellagen in **Bad**

Kreuznach and **Schlossbockelheim** produce fine Riesling wines. The wines are a bridge between the Mosel and Rhine in style; crisp yet elegant, with some body.

Baden

Baden is the most southerly of Germany's wine-growing regions, bordered by France to the west and Switzerland to the south. It is a diverse region, with a variety of different micro-climates, soils and grape varieties. Unfortunately the Baden wine one is most likely to come across is a fairly bland, medium-dry white, made by the ZBW Co-operative, which accounts for over 80 per cent of the wine produced in the region. A significant amount of red wine is produced in Baden from the Spätburgunder, as well as a popular rosé, **Weissherbst**.

Franken

Franken's vineyards lie along the river Main. The traditional Franconian wine is produced from Silvaner, vinified drier than most German wines, and bottled in a Bocksbeutel, a green, flagon-shaped bottle. These wines were often referred to as **Steinwein** after the famous Stein vineyard in Würzburg, centre of the wine-producing region. The majority of the wines produced today are from Müller-Thurgau.

The remaining six Anbaugebieten are not well known on export markets:

Ahr

The Ahr is Germany's northernmost wine region, but produces mainly red wines. This is because the vineyards are sited on the steep slopes of the river Ahr, which flows into the Rhine just south of Bonn, and are protected by the Hohe Eifel hills. The Spätburgunder and Portugieser produce light red wine and Weissherbst.

Mittelrhein

The Mittelrhein is the name given to the vineyards along the Rhein from Bonn south to Bingen. The steep vineyards bordering the river are mostly planted in Riesling, but the difficulty of working them has led to a decline in the number of growers, and most of the wine produced is consumed locally, particularly by tourists.

Hessische Bergstrasse

Hessische Bergstrasse lies to the east of the Rhine, north of Heidelberg. The mainly Riesling wines are more full-bodied and fruitier than the Rhine wines.

Württemberg

Württemberg produces fairly ordinary red wines, mainly from the Trollinger grape, grown on vineyards along the Neckar valley around Stuttgart. The pink **Schillerwein** is the region's speciality. There are a few good whites from Riesling as well.

Sachsen and Saale/Unstrut

Sachsen, the easternmost wine region of Germany, with vineyards along the Elbe valley, north of Dresden, and Saale/Unstrut, with vineyards along the two rivers of the same names, are two new Anbaugebiete from the former East Germany, producing mostly wines from Müller-Thurgau, but of little commercial interest at the moment.

CHAPTER FIVE

THE WINES OF ITALY

Italy, together with France, is the largest producer of wine in the world, with an average annual production of 60 million hectolitres. The first vineyards in Italy were probably planted by Greek settlers, and their reputation was such that the country became known as Oenotria – land of wine.

With a long history of political fragmentation and a variance in latitude of 10° between north and south, it is not surprising that Italy has a vast range of different styles of wine. More types of vines are planted in Italy than in any other country, including an enormous number of indigenous varieties capable of producing classic wines, as well as the ubiquitous imported vines.

Historically, much of Italy's wine was produced for local consumption, which gave little incentive to strive for quality. Most Italian wine was produced with the local cuisine in mind. Even today, with increasing exports, many Italian wines do not stand up well in comparative tastings, but achieve perfection when matched with food.

Much of the wine exported over the last 30 years has been in the cheap and cheerful mode – 2-litre bottles of Soave, Valpolicella and Lambrusco. However, there has also been a movement towards innovation and experiment by many leading producers and wine-makers, and a wide variety of exciting wines are now being made in Italy, albeit many of them in small quantities. Ironically, these developments have been as much hindered as helped by the regulations of the Italian Wine Laws.

Italian Wine Laws

The first laws, introduced in 1963, were intended to provide some unifying influence over the myriad different Italian wines. Despite subsequent changes and amendments, culminating with the Goria Law in 1992, many of Italy's finest wines fall outside the quality denominations, because they do not conform with the traditions of the region in which they are produced. The four levels of quality are, in descending order:

Denominazione di Origine Controllata e Garantita (DOCG) A higher grade than DOC below; these wines must be bottled in the region of production, are subject to tasting and must carry a seal of approval of the Ministry of Agriculture. So far only 13 DOCGs have been approved.

Denominazione di Origine Contrallata (DOC) The equivalent of the French Appellation Contrôlée system, regulating the area of production, grape varieties, yields, etc. There are now 240 DOC delimited areas, producing 900 different wines. Despite this, DOC and DOCG account for only 15 per cent of the total production in Italy.

Italy

Indicazione Geographica Tipica (IGT) A category introduced in the 1992 law which corresponds to the French Vin de Pays. The aim is to include the better Vini da Tavola which may indicate a specific area of production and/or grape variety.

Vino da Tavola The simplest denomination, with only limited controls over production, and without indication of origin.

The geography of Italy is dominated by mountains. The Alps and the Dolomites in the north give protection to the vineyards on their southern slopes. The climate north of the Po Valley is continental, with cold winters and long, warm summers. The Appennines, which form the backbone of Italy, provide the altitude to give cooler growing conditions in the centre and south of the country. Here the climate is typically Mediterranean, with warm winters and hot, dry summers.

Useful Terms

abboccato slightly sweet
amabile medium-sweet
amarone dry
annata vintage year
azienda agricola/agraria/vitivinicola estate making wine predominantly from its own vineyards
azienda/casa vinicola company making wine predominantly from bought-in grapes or wine

bianco white

botte cask

cantina cellar or winery

cantina sociale Co-operative winery

cerasuolo cherry-coloured rosé wine

chiaretto deeply coloured rosé

classico the central, historic zone of a denomination

consorzio consortium of producers

dolce sweet

fattoria/podere/tenuta farm or estate

frizzante slightly sparkling

invecchiato aged

metodo classico sparkling wine made by bottle-fermentation

recioto wine made from partly dried grapes; usually sweet

riserva wine aged for a specific (and longer) time

rosato rosé

rosso red

secco dry

spumante sparkling wine

uva grape

vendemmia harvest or vintage

vigna/vigneto vineyard

vino novello wine bottled in the year of harvest

vin santo sweet, dessert wine

Italy is divided into 20 political regions, all of which
produce wine. Starting in the north-west corner they are:

Valle D'Aosta

The smallest region, lying in the foothills of the Alps, nearly all of whose wines are consumed locally.

Piedmont

Literally meaning 'the foot of the mountains', Piedmont has more DOC and DOCG wines than any other region. The two most important areas of production are in the Langhe and Monferrato hills, around the towns of Alba and Asti, south-east of Turin, and north-east in the foothills of the Alps, near Lake Maggiore. The region enjoys warm, dry summers but the winters are cold with plenty of snow; vintage time is usually cool and often foggy.

The premier red wines of Piedmont are **Barolo** and **Barbaresco**, produced from the Nebbiolo grape grown in the Langhe hills. The wines have great concentration of flavour and are high in alcohol and tannin; in the past many were criticized for lacking fruit and elegance. The required minimum of 2 years' ageing in large oak casks for Barolo, one year for Barbaresco, usually following protracted maceration on the skins, often led to wines that tasted hard and astringent. However, many growers are now making wines with more balance, using shorter maceration, retaining the rich, chewy fruit flavour of the Nebbiolo. Barbaresco, which is grown in a lighter soil on gentler slopes, is generally less heavy and lower in alcohol than Barolo. A lesser denomination from the area is **Nebbiolo d'Alba**.

Other Piedmontese wines from the Nebbiolo grape are **Gattinara** and **Ghemme**, from near Lake Maggiore, where it is known as the Spanna, and **Carema**, from vineyards on the Swiss border.

Another indigenous red grape variety, the **Barbera**, traditionally produced fresh, fruity red wines for drinking young but some producers are today making more complex wines capable of ageing. The DOCs for Barbera are based on Alba, Asti and Monferrato. **Dolcetto** is another red variety that produces mostly soft, supple wines, but which some growers turn into a more concentrated wine, particularly in the DOC area of Alba. Three other local red varieties are Brachetto, Freisa and Grignolino.

The best-known Piedmontese white wine is the sparkling **Asti Spumante**, made from the Moscato grape. The wine is very aromatic, grapey and sweet; residual sugar is retained in the wine by stopping the fermentation around 7–8° alcohol. A similar style of wine, **Moscato d'Asti** is only lightly sparkling – *frizzante* – but with the same grapiness. Both these wines have now been accorded DOCG status.

Of the Piedmontese still white wines, **Gavi** is the best known. Produced from the Cortese grape, it is dry and full-flavoured with a crisp acidity.

Liguria

This narrow seaside region, south of Piedmont, produces only a small quantity of wine, most of which is drunk along the Italian Riviera.

Lombardy

Lying to the east of Piedmont, Lombardy produces fine Nebbiolo-based wines in **Valtellina**, a DOC area in the Alpine foothills, bordering Switzerland. To the south, the DOC region of **Franciacorta** produces good red and white wine, but is particularly well known for sparkling wine, made by bottle-fermentation, principally from Pinot Bianco grapes with some Chardonnay. **Oltrepo Pavese**, south of the river Po, produces a large amount of both red and white wine, from a variety of grapes, although only a small percentage achieves DOC status. On the western side of Lake Garda the red **Riviera del Garda** and white **Lugana** can compete respectably with the better-known Valpolicella and Soave from the opposite bank in the Veneto.

Veneto

The Veneto produces the largest quantity of DOC wine of all Italy's 20 regions. By far the best-known wines are the three produced in the province of Verona – **Soave**, **Valpo-**

licella and **Bardolino**. Soave is produced around the town of that name from the Garganega grape, with some Trebbiano; though generally light and dry, examples from the best sites in the *classico* area can show real depth and character. **Bianco di Custoza** and **Gambellara** are two other white DOCs very similar to Soave.

Valpolicella, produced from Corvina, Rondinella and Molinara grapes grown in the hills north of Verona, is generally known as a fresh, fruity red for drinking young. However, far more complex wines are produced by partly drying the ripest grapes prior to fermentation to produce deep, richly alcoholic wines. Those labelled as **Amarone della Valpolicella** are fermented totally dry, while **Recioto della Valpolicella** retains some sugar, and is one of the finest unfortified sweet red wines.

Bardolino, produced from the same grapes as Valpolicella, grown on the eastern side of Lake Garda, is a light and fruity red, often with a distinctive almond flavour.

A large quantity of varietal wines are also produced in the Veneto region. North of Venice, under the DOC of **Piave**, there are red wines, particularly Merlot and Cabernet (mostly Franc but some Sauvignon), and, increasingly, whites from Pinot Grigio, Sauvignon Blanc and Chardonnay.

Prosecco di Conegliano-Valdobbiadene is a slightly sweet, sparkling wine produced by tank-fermentation in the hills north-west of Venice around the towns of the same names.

Friuli-Venezia Giulia

This region in the very north-east of Italy, bordering Slovenia, produces many of the finest modern Italian white wines. The three principal DOCs are **Grave del Friuli**, the largest, **Colli Orientali del Friuli** and **Collio Goriziano**, or Collio. Traditional local varieties such as Tocai Friulano, Verduzzo and Ribolla, as well as Pinot Grigio and Bianco, Riesling and Chardonnay are usually sold as single varietals. **Picolit** produces a rare dessert wine.

Trentino-Alto Adige

The northernmost Italian region, bordering Switzerland and Austria; the province of Alto Adige is officially bilingual and is referred to as the Sudtirol by the German-speaking population. The Schiava grape produces light, fruity reds, the best of which are the DOCs of **Santa Maddalena** and **Lago di Caldaro**. Teroldego and Lagrein are two other local red varieties (**Teroldego Rotaliano** DOC is considered the finest); Cabernet and Merlot are also widely grown. The region produces many varietal wines under the DOCs of **Trentino** and **Alto Adige** or Sudtirol. The most successful are whites from Gewürztraminer, Chardonnay, Pinot Grigio and Bianco, Riesling, Sauvignon and Moscato.

Emilia-Romagna

Emilia-Romagna is the home of Lambrusco, made from the grape of that name. The semi-sweet, low-alcohol style in a screw-top bottle which is widely exported, as simply Vino da Tavola, bears little resemblance to the four DOC zones, east of Bologna, the best-known of which is **Lambrusco di Sorbara**. These wines are purple in colour, dry, slightly sparkling – *frizzante* – with a pronounced acidity – an ideal balance to the traditionally rich food of the area.

The region also produces the first DOCG white wine, **Albana di Romagna**, made from the grape of that name; it can be either dry or sweet, but cannot be said to justify its exalted position. Other wines from the same area, east of Bologna, are made from Trebbiano and Sangiovese, but the latter is a different clone to that in Tuscany.

Tuscany

The straw flask of Chianti was for many years the image of Italian wines. Today, much has changed and **Chianti** is one of Italy's 11 DOCGs. There are 7 distinct districts within the Chianti DOCG, the best-known being **Chianti Classico**, the central zone lying between Florence and Siena; the others are **Colle Aretini**, **Colle Fiorentini**, **Colli Senesi**, **Coline Pisane**, **Montalbano** and **Rufina**.

The principal grape variety for Chianti is the Sangiovese, specifically the superior clone Sangiovese Grosso, or Sangioveto, accounting for over 75 per cent; Canaiolo Nero and the white Trebbiano and Malvasia grapes are also allowed. In such a large area with significant variations in altitude, there are many different styles of Chianti. Some producers still use the practice known as *governo*, whereby the wine undergoes a slight secondary fermentation as a result of the addition of must from partly dried grapes. This accelerates the ageing and softens and rounds out the wine for drinking early. Riserva wines must be aged for 3 years. Traditionally wines were aged in large oak casks, *botti*; today many producers are also using small *barriques*.

Many producers of Chianti are also making high-quality Vini da Tavola, which because of the introduction of other grape varieties, particularly Cabernet-Sauvignon, do not meet the regulations for DOCG. None the less, the resulting wines are some of Italy's finest – Antinori's Tignanello began the trend.

Brunello di Montalcino   Also DOCG, this can equally be regarded as Tuscany's finest red wine. The Brunello is a clone of the Sangiovese, and produces a very concentrated wine, that must be aged for 4 years, 5 for Riserva.

Vino Nobile di Montepulciano   Italy's first DOCG is made from another Sangiovese clone, Prugnolo, and is very similar in style to a superior Chianti.

Carmignano   Tuscany's fourth DOCG; up to 10 per cent Cabernet-Sauvignon can be added to Sangiovese, but production of this red wine is very small.

Sassicaia Produced at San Guido on the Tuscan coast from 100 per cent Cabernet-Sauvignon grapes, this is considered one of Italy's finest red wines, but is only a Vino da Tavola.

Vernaccia di San Gimignano Tuscany's best-known white wine was in the past often heavy and oxidized, but is nowadays more often vinified in a crisp, fresh style.

Vin Santo Another speciality of Tuscany is this sweet dessert wine, made from semi-dried grapes and fermented slowly in small oak casks which are not topped up; it thus acquires a slightly oxidized as well as sweet taste.

Umbria

Orvieto Historically the best-known white wine from Umbria. Traditionally vinified with some residual sugar, *abboccato*, it is now being generally sold as a dry wine, from the same grape varieties – Trebbiano, Malvasia and Grechetto.

Torgiano A red wine made from the same grapes as Chianti, the Riserva version of which has become a DOCG. The same status has also been accorded the far less well-known **Sagrantino di Montefalco**.

The Marches

This region is home to **Verdicchio**, a dry white wine from the grape of the same name, often bottled in an amphora-shaped bottle. The best-known DOC area is the **Verdicchio dei Castelli di Jesi**, and with modern vinification techniques, the quality is improving.

There are two important red DOC areas, **Rosso Conero** and **Rosso Piceno**, which are produced from Montepulciano and Sangiovese grapes.

Abruzzi

This region has just two DOCs: red **Montepulciano d'Abruzzo** and white **Trebbiano d'Abruzzo**.

Lazio

Lazio is the home of **Frascati**, produced from Malvasia and Trebbiano grapes grown in the hills south-east of Rome. The light, fresh, dry white wine produced today owes much to improvements in vinification techniques.

Molise

This region has only two DOCs, **Biferno** and **Pentro**, which remain relatively unknown.

Campania

The hills east of Naples are the home of Campania's three best wines. **Taurasi** is a DOCG red wine, made from the

Aglianico grape; rich and tannic, it needs time to develop. **Greco di Tufo** and **Fiano di Avellino** are both white DOCs made from the grapes of the same name. They are both local varieties producing wines of much more character than the ubiquitous Trebbiano.

Puglia

This region forms the heel of Italy and has the largest production of any region although less than 2 per cent is of DOC status. Two red wines of more than local interest are the DOCs of **Castel del Monte** and **Salice Salentino**.

Basilicata

There is just one DOC, the red, of note in this region: **Aglianico del Vulture**.

Calabria

Two DOCs are worthy of note: **Ciro Rosso** from the Gaglioppo grape and **Greco di Bianco**, a sweet white from the grape of the same name.

Sicily

Sicily is Italy's largest region, with more land under vine than any other area, and production second only to Puglia, although only 2 ½ per cent is of DOC status, and most of that is **Marsala** (see Chapter 7). There are, however, some good Vini da Tavola, made predominantly from local grapes, which are recognized by the region's own quality seal of approval, shown as a Q on the label.

Very fine Moscato is produced on the island of Pantelleria, off the south-west coast.

Sardinia

The majority of Sardinian wines are named after the grape variety from which they are produced; red Cannonau, related to the Grenache, can be sweet or dry; Vermentino and Nuragus are the most widely planted white varieties.

CHAPTER SIX

THE WINES OF
IBERIA

SPAIN

Spain has more land under vine than any other country in the world. Between the Pyrenees that form the frontier with France in the north and the Straits of Gibraltar just 15 km from the African coast in the south, Spain boasts over a million hectares of vineyard. But yields are often pathetically low, reflecting the extreme conditions that prevail throughout much of the country where drought is a common problem. Total production in the early 1990s averaged 35 million hectolitres, making Spain the world's fourth largest wine producer after France, Italy and the former Soviet Union.

Spain is a large and diverse country with great mountain ranges dividing the Iberian land mass into distinct regions, some of which behave almost like nation states in their own right. Galicia and the Basque Country, each with their own language and culture on the cool green northern Atlantic coast, seem to have little in common with arid Castile or Mediterranean Andalusia to the south. The Spanish constitution recognizes this, dividing the state into 16 autonomous regions and one principality, each with its own regional government.

Iberia's salient physical feature is the high plateau known

as the *meseta* that occupies much of central Spain. Here the climate is cruel. Winters are long and cold, with temperatures falling well below freezing. Summers are dry and hot, with daytime temperatures frequently rising above 40°C. Irrigation is forbidden under legislation from the EC, and grape varieties like the white Airen and red Garnacha are planted to withstand the harsh physical conditions. Towards the coastal regions, the climate becomes more equable. The Atlantic coast to the north and west is relatively cool and damp, with rainfall reaching 2000 mm on some of the higher mountain ranges. South and east from the central *meseta*, the climate is increasingly influenced by the Mediterranean where summers are warm and winters are mild.

Spain's regional differences are reflected in its wines, which range from delicate, dry, cool-climate whites in the north to heavy alcoholic reds throughout the south, and rich fortified wines in Andalusia of which sherry is the most famous example (see Chapter 7). Over the past two decades, Spain's wine industry has benefited from significant improvements in wine technology. Temperature-controlled fermentation in stainless steel, which is essential for red and white wine in a hot climate, has become widespread. The programme of investment initiated in the late 1970s has been helped by Spain's accession to the EC together with Portugal in 1986.

Since joining the EC, Spain's wine laws have been brought roughly into line with those of other member

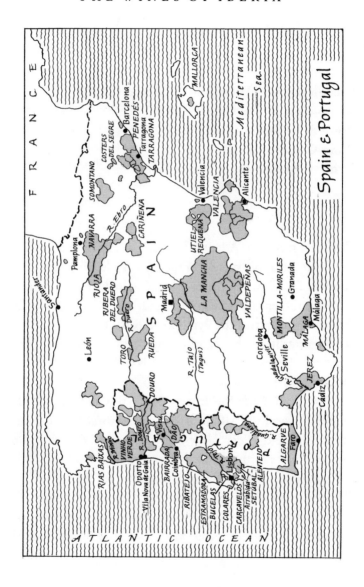

Spain & Portugal

states. There are now 5 tiers to the pyramid (from the top downwards), as follows:

Denominacion de Origen Calificada (DOC)
Denominacion de Origen (DO)
Vino de la Tierra (VdlT)
Vino Comarcal (VC)
Vino de Mesa (VdM) (Table Wine)

Rioja

Shielded from the Atlantic by the Cantabrian mountains, Rioja, in the upper section of the Ebro Valley, is Spain's best known DOC wine region. It benefited from the late-nineteenth-century phylloxera epidemic which drove the French south across the Pyrenees to Rioja in search of wine. They introduced the 225-litre oak cask or *barrique* (now known in Spain as a *barrica*) which is still used for maturing the region's finest wines.

Named after the Rio (river) Oja, a tiny tributary of the mighty river Ebro, Rioja divides into three sub-regions. Rioja Alta and Rioja Alavesa in the higher and therefore cooler reaches of the valley are planted predominantly with Tempranillo, Spain's finest indigenous red grape variety. Further south and east, in Rioja Baja, the hotter, more arid country downstream from the regional capital Logroño, the chief grape is the Garnacha. Most Riojas are blends from all three districts, with Garnacha lending body to the lighter and finer Tempranillo. All but the plainest red wines spend a certain amount of time ageing in *barricas* made from American oak. Wines labelled Crianza spend a minimum of 6 months in *barrica*, Reservas spend a year and Gran Reservas selected from the best harvests are aged in cask for at least 2 years before bottling. As the wine ages it softens, losing harsh tannins and taking on the smooth, vanilla-like character of the oak which is the hallmark of a fine red Rioja.

A few white wines made from Viura and Malvasia grapes are also aged in *barrica*, but the recent trend has been towards fruitier, early-bottled wines made without recourse to oak.

Navarra

DO Navarra adjoins Rioja Baja and makes similarly full, sometimes coarse, oak-aged reds and dry, fruity rosés from the Garnacha grape. Newer vineyards planted with Tempranillo and Cabernet-Sauvignon are helping to refine the Navarra's red wines.

Ribera del Duero

This DO wine region on the banks of the river Duero in Old Castile looks set to challenge Rioja as Spain's leading producer of red wines. Since the nineteenth century it has been home to Bodegas Vega Sicilia, Spain's equivalent of a first growth which languished on its own for over 100 years. Other producers are now making dark, dense, oak-aged reds from the Tinto Fino and Tinto del Pais grapes, both local variants of Rioja's Tempranillo.

Toro

This smaller DO downstream from Ribera del Duero makes similarly dark, though coarser, reds from the Tinto de Toro grape (alias Tempranillo).

Rueda

This DO region between Ribera del Duero and Toro produces refreshing dry white wines from the perfumed Verdejo grape. A few traditional *bodegas* continue to make coarse fortified wines from Palomino, the grape variety used to produce sherry.

Galicia

Galicia being the coolest and wettest part of Spain, its collection of DO wine regions produce light, dry white wines, many of which share a similarity with Portugal's Vinhos Verdes. The coastal *denominacion* **Rias Baixas** is best known for its fragrant white wines made from the highly prized Albarino grape. Inland, the DOs of **Valdeorras** and **Ribeiro** tend to make stronger whites and simple rustic reds.

Catalonia

Centred on Spain's second-largest city Barcelona, Catalonia is home to Spain's thriving sparkling wine industry. The *méthode champenoise* (see Chapter 3), which was first introduced to the small Catalan town of San Sadurni de Noya in the nineteenth century, is now known in Spain as **Cava** (an official denominacion de Origen in its own right). Two firms, Codorniu and Freixenet, are now among the largest sparkling wine producers in the world.

Among the other regional DOs in Catalonia, **Penedès**, rising in a series of steps from the Mediterranean south-west of Barcelona, is much the most important for both quantity and quality. Among the large wine-makers, the family firm of Torres was at the centre of a revolution in Spanish wine-making in the 1970s and 1980s. Apart from Tempranillo and the trio of white grapes used in the making of Cava, there are significant vineyards planted with French varieties like Cabernet-Sauvignon and Chardonnay.

La Mancha

South of Madrid, the national capital strategically sited in the heart of the country, **La Mancha** is the world's largest demarcated vineyard region. An ocean of vines stretches as far as the eye can see across the *meseta*, producing large quantities of dry white wine from the Airen grape, mainly for the local market. The Airen is not just the most planted grape in Spain, it is also the most planted variety in the world. Modern temperature-controlled vinification has helped to improve quality in the scorching climate here, but the bulk of La Mancha's wine is made for distillation.

Valdepeñas

This is an enclave just to the south of La Mancha making soft, oak-aged reds from the Tempranillo grape, posing under the name Cencibel.

The Levante

In the hills behind the holiday Costas, wine plays an important part in the rural economy. Red wines predominate, made from Bobal which sometimes ripens to give natural alcohol levels as high as 16–18°. The Mediterranean port of **Valencia** is also the name of the principal DO wine region.

Andalusia

The deep south is primarily fortified-wine country, but the wines of Montilla-Morilles, which resemble sherry, are made from super-ripe Pedro Ximenez grapes and achieve 16° of alcohol without fortification (see Chapter 7).

PORTUGAL

This small seafaring country on Europe's westernmost flank produces a remarkable diversity of wines. Roughly rectangular in shape, it is under 600 km long and no more than 200 km wide. The wines produced on the flat coastal plain are strongly influenced by the prevailing westerly winds from the Atlantic. The temperate maritime climate, with warm summers and cool, wet winters, becomes more extreme towards the south and east. As an illustration of this, rainfall which reaches 2000 mm on the northern hills diminishes to less than 500 mm in some inland wine regions.

Reflecting these contrasting climatic conditions, no two wines could be more dissimilar than port (see Chapter 7) and Vinho Verde, both of which are produced in the north of Portugal in adjoining regions. There are pockets of viticulture all over Portugal. From the River Minho in the north to the Algarve in the south there are over 350,000 hectares of vineyard producing an annual average of 8 million hectolitres of wine. North of the River Tagus the country is dominated by smallholders, most of whom deliver their grapes to one of over 120 co-operative wineries. In complete contrast, the land south of the Tagus is divided into large private estates, some of which extend to many hundreds of hectares.

Portugal's vineyards have evolved in virtual isolation, with only a handful of vines having crossed international frontiers. Internationally recognized varieties like Cabernet-Sauvignon and Chardonnay have made few inroads, leaving Portugal with a wealth of native grapes. Among the best red grapes are Touriga Naçional (in the Douro and Dão), Baga (in Bairrada) and Castelão Frances (also known as Periquita) which is planted widely throughout the south. Among the most promising white varieties are Loureiro and Alvarinho (both in Vinho Verde), Arinto (in Bucelas) and Fernão Pires (throughout the south).

Portugal lays claim to one of the first delimited regions in the world: the Douro valley was demarcated as early as 1756. A number of other regions were awarded **Região Demarcada** (demarcated region) status in the early twentieth century. Since Portugal joined the EC in 1986, the country's wine law has been substantially revised to bring it into line with the rest of Europe. There are four tiers of wine region, roughly equivalent to the French AC/VDQS/Vin de Pays Vin de Table, as follows:

Denominação de Origem (DOC)
Indicação de Proveniencia Regulamentada (IPR)
Vinho Regional
Vinho de Mesa (Table Wine)

Vinho Verde

The largest and northernmost of Portugal's DOCs, the Vinho Verde region is strongly influenced by its proximity to the Atlantic. The relatively cool, damp climate, granite-based soils and vigorous, high-yielding vines combine to produce wines which tend to be low in alcohol and high in acidity, bottled to retain a little carbon dioxide gas. Paradoxically, Vinho Verde (meaning 'green wine') may be either red or white, but very little red is exported, its astringency being something of an acquired taste. With the notable exception of a number of single-estate wines, Vinho Verde rarely displays a vintage date on the label. It is accepted that the wine should be drunk within a year of the harvest, hence the name 'green' or young. In the extreme north of the region around the town of Monção, Alvarinho grapes are used to produce a highly prized varietal Vinho Verde with more body and depth of flavour.

Douro

Known primarily for port, the steeply terraced vineyards of the Douro Valley were demarcated for light wine in 1979. Depending on the size of the harvest, around half the region's production is not fortified for port but fermented out to produce full-bodied red and white wines. With the advent of new wine-making techniques, Douro reds, which were criticized for being hard and tannic, are becoming softer and more approachable. Grape varieties like Touriga Nacional and Tinta Roriz (alias Tempranillo in Spain) are capable of producing some good, ripe-flavoured red wines.

Dão

Locked in by granite mountains in the heart of northern Portugal, Dão is capable of producing some of the country's best wines. The region is dominated by large co-operative wineries, and standards tended to slip in the 1960s and 1970s: too many red wines are mean and astringent through excessive ageing in bulk and in bottle. A number of private wine producers, in particular Sogrape, Portugal's largest wine-makers, have invested in modern wineries, and the quality of red and white Dão is gradually improving. Touriga Naçional, along with indigenous grapes like Tinta Pinheira, Jaen and Bastardo, produce some solid reds. Encruzado, the best grape for white Dão, is used to make some fragrant dry white wines.

Bairrada

This coastal DOC on fertile clay soils south of Oporto produces dark, tannic red wines from the Baga grape which traditionally required extended ageing. With modern vinification techniques, a number of producers are making softer, earlier-maturing wines. White grapes produce about 10 per cent of the region's wine, most of which is used by the local sparkling wine industry.

Oeste/Estremadura

The largest wine region in Portugal in terms of volume, this group of 6 IPRs north of Lisbon tends to produce quantity rather than quality. Only a handful of single estates around Alenquer are worthy of note.

Colares

This small DOC region on the coast north-west of Lisbon is unique for its phylloxera-free vines growing in sandy soils. Firm, fragrant red wines from the Ramisco grape are highly prized but increasingly rare as production costs have escalated in recent years.

Bucelas

This small DOC region produces white wines from the Arinto and Esgana Cão ('dog strangler') grapes north-east of Lisbon.

Ribatejo

Second only to the Oeste Estremadura in terms of volume, the fertile alluvial soils alongside the River Tagus (Tejo) produce inexpensive dry whites and fruity reds.

Setúbal Peninsula

Between the Tagus and Sado estuaries south of Lisbon, the Setúbal Peninsula is the home of two of Portugal's most innovative wine-makers, Jose Maria da Fonseca and J. P. Vinhos. Two IPRs, Arrabida and Palmela, produce wines ranging from modern, cool-fermented dry whites to full-flavoured oak-aged reds. This is one of the few areas of

Portugal where foreign grapes like Cabernet-Sauvignon and Chardonnay grow alongside native varieties, in particular the Castelão Frances or Periquita. Many wines are now labelled with the Vinho Regional name, Terras do Sado.

Alentejo

This broad, sun-baked plain south and east of Lisbon extends from the Atlantic coast to the Spanish border. Vineyards are gaining ground in the Alentejo, which is also one of the world's most important producers of cork. Eight IPR regions include Borba, Reguengos and Redondo, increasingly well-known for their big, ripe red wines, some of which are labelled as Vinho Regional – Alentejo. A number of Australian wine-makers have had an important bearing on the style of wines from Alentejo, most of which tend to be made with native grapes, the best of which are the white Fernão Pires and Roupeiro and the red Castelão Frances, Trincadeira and Aragonez.

Algarve

Demarcated in 1980, the Algarve is better known for its beaches than for the quality of its red and white wines, which tend to reflect the hot oceanic summers.

CHAPTER SEVEN

FORTIFIED WINES

Fortified wines are so called because they are bolstered or 'fortified' by the addition of alcohol, mostly in the form of brandy or grape spirit. The alcohol may be added after the fermentation, producing a dry wine like a fino sherry, or it may be added during the fermentation, thereby arresting it and producing a sweet wine like port. Many of the world's great fortified wines evolved almost by accident from the days when wines had to endure long sea journeys to reach their destination. It then became the normal practice to add a small amount of brandy to stabilize the wine, thereby preventing it from re-fermenting in cask. Fortified wines became very fashionable in the late eighteenth and nineteenth centuries, but their overall popularity has since waned in favour of lighter styles. However, there are three great fortified wines – sherry, port and madeira, all of which have retained substantial markets world-wide.

SHERRY

Sherry is the English corruption of the Spanish name 'Jerez', from the city of Jerez de la Frontera in Spain. It has also become a generic term applied to a number of fortified wines made in other countries, notably Cyprus, South Africa and Australia, although moves have been made within the EC to restrict the use of the term 'sherry' to wines from the Jerez region.

All real sherry, therefore, comes from the official Jerez Denomination of Origin (DO), which covers rolling limestone hills in Andalusia, in south-west Spain. The best vineyards are located on brilliant white calcareous soils known as *albariza*, which are found in between the inland city of Jerez de la Frontera and the coastal towns of Sanlucar de Barrameda and El Puerto de Santa Maria. Proximity to the Atlantic plays an important part in both the cultivation of grapes and, more importantly, the maturation of the wine.

The principal sherry grape, accounting for over 90 per cent of the vineyard area, is the Palomino Fino which grows elsewhere in Spain but tends to produce undistinguished neutral dry wines. The Pedro Ximenez grape which is prolific in neighbouring Montilla is now of limited importance in Jerez and tends to be found growing in the heavier soils. A small amount of Moscatel (Muscat) is also planted in the sandy coastal areas where it produces wines for blending and sweetening.

There are two principal styles of sherry: pale dry **fino** and dark, full but dry **oloroso**. The classification and selection of these wines begins at an early stage. Wines destined to become finos are sourced from the best calcareous *albariza* soils. Wines destined to be olorosos come from grapes grown on the heavier clays.

The harvest begins in September when the grapes, which were once trodden by foot, are crushed and the juice is fermented in modern stainless steel wineries. A few traditional producers continue to ferment in cask or butt. Almost all the wines are fermented to dryness so that all the natural grape sugar turns to alcohol. The resulting Palomino base wine is therefore a rather bland dry white wine with around 11° of alcohol.

The second classification takes place soon after the end of the fermentation. Wines destined to develop into pale dry finos are fortified with colourless grape spirit known as *aguardiente* to an alcohol level of 15–15.5°. Casks known as *botas* or 'butts' are then partially filled, and a film of yeast known as *flor* develops on the surface. This protects the wine from oxidation as it ages. The growth of *flor* is responsible for the characteristic bread-like aroma and tang of a delicate, dry fino sherry or manzanilla, distinguishing these from other styles of sherry. *Flor* is inhibited by an alcoholic strength much above 16°. Wines destined to develop into olorosos which age without *flor* are therefore fortified to a higher strength of around 18° and the casks or butts are completely filled to the bung-hole.

All styles of sherry are aged in a *solera*. This is a system of fractional blending which helps to refresh and nurture the *flor* in finos and maintains a consistent style for other sherry categories. For this reason a bottle of sherry never displays a vintage on the label. A sherry *solera* is made up of a number of levels or tiers, each of which is known as a *criadera*. Wine withdrawn for bottling from the bottom tier called the *solera* is replenished from the first *criadera*, which is in turn replenished from the second *criadera* and so on in a process known as running the scales. The whole system is fed by wine from the most recent harvest, known as *añada*. A *solera* may vary in size from just a few butts to many thousands. The famous Tio Pepe *solera* belonging to Gonzalez Byass is made up of around 30,000 butts.

The many different styles of sherry all evolve from the two main categories, fino and oloroso, as follows:

Fino   Pale, dry sherry aged under a film of *flor* yeast at Jerez de la Frontera. Should be served chilled in partially filled tulip-shaped glasses known as *copitas*. Good to drink in Spain with the bite-sized snacks known as *tapas* or with seafood.

Manzanilla   Very delicate, pale dry style of fino aged under *flor* yeast at Sanlucar de Barrameda on the coast. *Flor* is very sensitive to heat and therefore grows more thickly and evenly in the cooler maritime climate. Serve like a fino.

Pale Cream   A coarse fino which has been sweetened with concentrated grape must. Serve well chilled.

Amontillado   An old fino which has lost its protective covering of *flor* and therefore turns an amber colour, changing character in contact with the air. Amontillados are naturally dry, with a pungent aroma and a characteristic nutty tang, but many commercial examples are sweetened. Serve at room temperature on its own before a meal or with soup.

Oloroso   Dark, rich and raisiny but naturally dry. Sweet olorosos (Oloroso Dulce) are made by blending with intensely sweet, dark wines made from sun-dried Pedro Ximenez grapes. Serve the dry wine at room temperature as an apéritif or sweet oloroso after a meal with nuts and dried fruit in place of port.

Cream   Another name for a sweet oloroso, often used for commercial brands.

Palo Cortado   A style in between an oloroso and amontillado, now rarely seen.

PORT

Port derives its name from Portugal's second largest city, Oporto (Porto), from where the wine (Vinho do Porto) has been shipped for over 300 years, although port-style wines are also made in Australia, California and South Africa. The city of Oporto, on the estuary of the River Douro, is separate from the port vineyards which are situated either side of the river in wild, mountainous country some 50 miles upstream.

The Douro Valley was the first major wine region in the world to receive an official demarcation. Recognizing the unique physical characteristics of the region, in 1756

Portugal's Prime Minister the Marques de Pombal drew a boundary around the Douro, restricting the production of port to vineyards within the demarcation. It predates other demarcated wine regions by more than a century.

Pombal's demarcation, modified a number of times since the eighteenth century, corresponds closely to an outcrop of slate-like rock known as schist. The soils are poor and hard to cultivate but over the years the land has been worked to great advantage. Tiny terraces have been carved from the steep, craggy slopes overlooking the River Douro, each supporting a few rows of vines. Although the area is protected from the Atlantic by a range of mountains to the west and rainfall diminishes sharply towards the Spanish border in the east, the climate is harsh, with long, hot summers and bitterly cold winters. It is hard to imagine a more inhospitable place to grow grapes.

The Douro is officially subdivided into 3 zones for the production of port: **Baixo Corgo** in the west, **Cima Corgo** in the centre and **Douro Superior** to the east. The best wines tend to originate from the Cima Corgo, recognized by a complex classification system which grades individual vineyards from A to F according to the potential quality of the wine. This determines the proportion of the crop from an individual property that may be made into port. The remainder is made into light wine which has its own regional demarcation (see Chapter 6).

As many as 80 different grape varieties are authorized for the production of port, but over recent years research has identified 5 as being of outstanding quality: **Touriga Nacional**, **Tinta Barroca**, **Touriga Francesa**, **Tinta Roriz** and **Tinto Cão**. The harvest usually begins in late September and the wines are vinified in the region. After picking and crushing, fermentation begins in much the same way as for any red wine. However, when approximately half the natural grape sugar has fermented to alcohol, the wine is run off and fortified with *aguardiente*. The spirit kills off the active yeasts in the wine, thereby arresting the fermentation and leaving the wine rich in natural sugar. The main problem with this short fermentation is in obtaining sufficient colour, extract and tannin from the skins of the grapes before fortification. The traditional method involves treading the grapes with the human foot, but larger producers have resorted to mechanical methods.

Most of the new wine stays in the Douro for the winter after the harvest before being transported downstream to the city of Vila Nova da Gaia which faces Oporto on the opposite side of the river estuary. Here the major port shippers own long, low buildings known as *armazens*, or lodges, where the wines age in a variety of wooden vessels including 550-litre casks called *pipas*, or pipes. The relatively cool, humid coastal climate is considered ideal for maturation, which ultimately determines the style of the wine.

The main styles of port are as follows:

Ruby A blend of basic young, fruity wines aged for 2–3 years before bottling, so named because of its youthful colour. Dark and rich.

Vintage Character   Premium ruby port aged for between three and five years.

Tawny   Varies from young, light, pink wines to older wines with a true tawny colour and a smooth, silky character; youthful colour and tannin subside with age. The best tawnies are usually bottled with an indication of age: '10 Years Old', '20 Years Old', 'Thirty Years Old' and sometimes 'Over 40 Years Old'. These are not exact ages but merely indications corresponding to styles approved by the Port Wine Institute which oversees the trade.

Vintage   Rich, concentrated, powerful wine 'declared' by shippers after a single exceptional harvest. Vintage ports are bottled without any filtration after two to three years in wood. They spend a further 10 to 20 years in bottle before the wine is ready to drink. Vintage port throws a natural sediment in the bottle and has to be decanted before serving. Most shippers regard vintage port as their finest wine.

Late Bottled Vintage (LBV)   Wine from a single good, though not usually exceptional, year bottled between the fourth and sixth years after the harvest. It varies in style from large, commercial brands (some of which are little better than basic ruby) to rich, so-called 'traditional' LBVs, which are bottled without any filtration and should be decanted before serving.

Single Quinta   Wine from a single farm or *quinta*, usually from a single good year (although not a 'declared' vintage) and bottled like a vintage port.

Crusted or **Crusting**   A blend of high-quality wines from a number of years bottled without filtration so that the wine throws sediment, known as a 'crust', in the bottle. Decant before serving.

Colheita   A tawny port from a single year bottled after spending at least 7 years in wood.

White Port   Port made from white grapes.

MADEIRA

At first sight the Portuguese island of Madeira, 700 km from the coast of North Africa, seems an unlikely place to make wine. The climate is humid and sub-tropical and vineyards clamber up steep volcanic slopes which rise to a height of over 1800 m. Perpetual clouds cover the highest mountain peaks.

The island was discovered by the Portuguese in the fifteenth century and, as overseas trade developed, Madeira soon became an important staging post for ships *en route* for Africa and the East. They filled their empty holds with wine, adding alcohol in order to prevent it from spoiling during long voyages. It was discovered almost by chance that Madeira wine tasted better after pitching and rolling through the tropics, and markets developed in both Europe and North America for wine that had been shipped back and forth across the equator. By the nineteenth century, merchants began to simulate the effects of these long but costly tropical sea voyages by heating the wine in casks or vats known as *estufas*. This practice continues to the present day.

The bulk of Madeira, made from the Tinta Negra Mole grape, is heated to between 40 and 50°C for a minimum period of 90 days in a process known as *estufagem*. The heat accelerates the development of the wine, producing the characteristic maderized aromas and flavours. The finest madeiras are still made without any artificial heating. These wines, produced mainly from the four so-called 'noble' grapes, **Sercial**, **Verdelho**, **Bual** and **Malvasia**, are left to age in small casks stowed in naturally warm *armazens* in the island's capital, Funchal. Some wines spend 50 years or more in wood before they are bottled.

Until recently the different styles of Madeira were distinguished by the noble grape varieties from which the wines were originally made. Sercial produces the driest wine with a distinct tang; Verdelho is softer and medium-dry, Bual is medium-sweet and Malmsey or Malvasia makes the richest and most unctuous Madeira wine. But since Portugal joined the EC in 1986 the labelling of Madeira has been changed to comply with EC law. Madeira wine made from the versatile but inferior Tinta Negra Mole, which accounts for around 80 per cent of the island's production is now restricted to using the following terms: Seco (dry), Meio Seco (medium-dry), Meio Doce (medium-sweet) and Doce (sweet).

The age and quality of Madeira is generally indicated on the label as follows:

Finest   Basic blended wines approximately three years old.

Reserve   A blend of five-year-old wines.

Special Reserve   Ten-year-old wines usually made from noble varieties and aged without *estufagem*.

Solera   Similar in principle to the sherry *soleras* (see pages 159–60), although on Madeira the practice of ageing in *solera* is being discontinued.

Vintage   The very finest wines from a single year, bottled after spending at least 20 years in cask although most spend considerably longer. Once in bottle, vintage Madeiras may be kept almost indefinitely. Wines from the early nineteenth century are still in good condition.

OTHER FORTIFIED WINES

Spain

Malaga   Rich, raisiny fortified wines much appreciated in the UK in the nineteenth century.

Portugal

Setubal   Opulent wines made predominantly from Moscatel (Muscat).

Carcavelos   Rather rustic port-style wine, popular in the nineteenth century but now scarce.

Italy

Marsala   Fortified wine from Sicily varying in style from dry and nutty to rich and sweet.

Australia

Rutherglen Muscat   Intensely sweet fortified wine made from very ripe Muscat grapes, often allowed to dry out to raisins, in northern Victoria.

CHAPTER EIGHT

THE WINES OF CENTRAL AND SOUTH-EASTERN EUROPE

AUSTRIA

Austria is today producing increasing quantities of good-quality wine, following the so-called 'anti-freeze' scandal of 1985. In that year a number of wines were found to contain diethylene glycol, which had been added to hide the fact that extra sugar had been added to the wine illegally. (The reason for adding sugar is that wines with higher levels of 'natural' grape sugars command higher prices.) The scandal that followed effectively halted the country's exports, particularly the large quantities which went to Germany. It should be mentioned that only a few people were involved and the danger to health from diethylene glycol was probably less than from the natural alcohol in the wine. As a result the wine industry in Austria has had to rebuild itself, but now the emphasis is directed much more to quality than to quantity. The 1985 Austrian Wine Law sought to prevent future malpractice with tight controls.

The Austrian system of quality control follows that of Germany quite closely, but the minimum Oechsle levels (the specific gravity of the wine which indicates the sugar content) for each category are significantly higher. Tafelwein and Landwein may not be exported. Qualitätswein and Kabinett are of a higher grade and unlike Qualitätswein in Germany, neither may be chaptalized. Prädikatswein includes Spätlese, Auslese, Beerenauslese, Eiswein and Trockenbeerenauslese, and also Ausbruch. This last is a category requiring an Oechsle level between Beerenauslese and Trockenbeerenauslese, but the botrytized grapes are mixed with juice of Spätlese quality, which produces an intensely honeyed wine, but less rich. The maximum yields allowed in Austria are significantly lower than in Germany. All wines are tested and must show the Staatliche Prufnummer on the label.

Austria benefits from a warm, dry, continental climate, and so can produce wines with higher sugar levels more easily than Germany.

Eighty per cent of the wine produced in Austria is white. Grüner Veltliner is the most popular grape variety, accounting for over a third of all plantings. The wine it produces has a slightly smoky, spicy flavour and it is best drunk young. Müller-Thurgau, the second most widely planted variety, accounts for less than 10 per cent, and an important quantity of wine is also made from the Welschriesling, a different variety to the Rhine Riesling, but capable of producing above-average wines at Prädikatswein level. Blauer Portugieser and Zweigelt are the two most widely planted red varieties, although neither can be said to produce great wines. Small but increasing amounts of Cabernet-Sauvignon, Chardonnay and Pinot Noir are being planted.

The Austrian vineyards are all located in the east of the

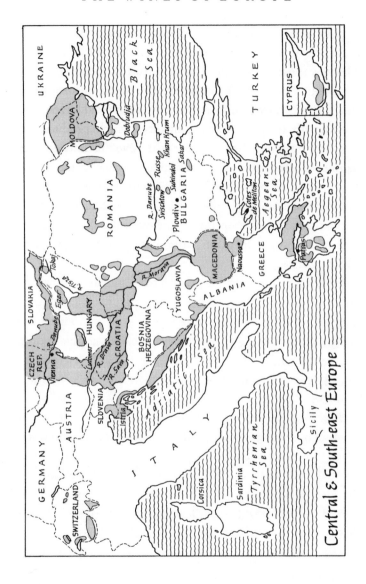

Central & South-east Europe

country, north and south of **Vienna**. The capital city itself is at the centre of a wine-growing region, the production of which is mostly consumed in the city's *Heurigen*, or wine bars. The region of **Niederösterreich**, north-west of Vienna, is best known for very good Grüner Veltliner and Riesling wines, particularly from the districts of Wachau and Kamtal-Donauland, around the town of Krems. The region of **Burgenland**, south of Vienna, includes the Neusiedler See, a shallow lake whose micro-climate creates the ideal conditions for botrytis, and therefore some fine, sweet white wines. **Styria**, in the very south-east of the country, is best known for a rosé wine, **Schilcher**, most of which is consumed locally.

BULGARIA

Bulgaria has become the fifth largest wine supplier to the United Kingdom. Its reputation has been built on well-priced, sound varietal wines, particularly the soft, rich and rounded Cabernet-Sauvignons.

The Bulgarian Wine Law of 1978 established different levels of quality; those which are seen on export markets are:

(a) Wines without designated geographic origin, which are usually sold under a brand name.

(b) Wines of **Declared Geographical Origin (DGO)** which come from a specified region which is indicated on the label. If described as a Country Wine it must be made from two grape varieties, otherwise these wines are single varietals. There are 119 areas so far designated as DGOs.

(c) **Controliran** wines are produced from specified grape varieties in certain DGOs, both of which must be shown on the label, and have to be passed by a tasting panel. Around 25 have so far been designated.

Reserve indicates that the wines have been aged in oak casks – in the case of DGOs 2 years for white wines, 3 for red, and for Controliran wines 3 years for white and 4 for red.

Special Reserve indicates white wines which have been barrel-fermented or red wines aged in new oak casks.

The best-known Cabernet-Sauvignon wines come from **Suhindol** and **Russe** in the Northern Region, and **Plovdiv**, **Oriahovica** and **Sakar Mountain** in the Southern Region. There are also interesting indigenous varieties: **Gamza** from Suhindol; **Mavrud** from Asenovgrad in the Southern Region and **Melnik** from the town of the same name and Harsovo in the South-west region. **Khan Krum** in the Eastern region is well known for its Chardonnay.

HUNGARY

Hungary's most famous wine is **Tokay**, or Tokaji, the sweetest variety of which was highly prized by the Tsars of Russia. It comes from the town of Tokaj, in the north-east of the country, where the misty autumns encourage the development of botrytis in the Furmint and Harslevelu grapes.

Tokay is produced in different styles. **Tokay Szamorodni** is made from grapes which have not become botrytized and is therefore dry or medium-dry. **Tokay Aszu** is made from botrytized grapes, and is sold by number of *puttonyos*, which indicate the degree of sweetness. *Puttony* is the name of the wooden hod used for harvesting the grapes. Botrytized grapes are put into these wooden tubs for a week; the minute quantity of juice that runs out naturally is known as *essencia*, which in the past was fabled as an elixir of life. Once this is run off, the grapes are pounded into a paste which is then added to casks of dry wine. The more *puttonyos* – tubs of paste – added, the sweeter the final wine; Tokay Aszu 3 *puttonyos* has a minimum 60 grams per litre residual sugar, 4 *puttonyos* 90 grams per litre, 5 puttonyos 120 grams per litre and 6 *puttonyos* 150 grams per litre. Tokay Aszu Essencia has over 200 grams per litre residual sugar. The wines are aged in 140-litre barrels, called *gonc*, which are not filled to the top, so that the wine slowly oxidizes as it ages – a minimum 4 years for 2 *puttonyos*, 8 years for 6 *puttonyos*.

The region of Eger, between Budapest and Tokay, is best known for **Bull's Blood**, Egri Bikaver, a red wine made from the Kadarka grape, whose quality fails to live up to its reputation. An increasing number of varietal wines are now being made, particularly Sauvignon and Chardonnay from Gyongyos, in the Matra hills.

The Hungarian version of Welschriesling, **Olaszrizling** is still widely planted, particularly in the Great Plain south of Budapest, as well as in the smaller regions around Pecs and Lake Balaton. The wines produced, whether dry, medium-dry or medium-sweet, are rarely exciting.

Sopron is a potentially fine wine area, which juts into Austria's Burgenland, in the north-west of the country. Traditionally the wines have been made from the Kekfrankos grape, but there are now plantings of Cabernet and Merlot.

With the exception of Tokay, the potential for Hungary's wines seems to lie more with the new varietal wines from classic grape varieties, vinified using modern equipment. With the increasing amount of external investment in equipment and expertise, allied to the natural climate and variety of soils, there is little doubt that there is a future for Hungarian wines on the world market.

ROMANIA

Romania is the largest wine-producing country in the Balkans. Its best-known wine is **Banat Riesling** from the west of the country, but the greatest potential probably exists in **Transylvania**, where crisp, fruity white wines are produced from Riesling, Pinot Gris, Sauvignon and the local Feteasca grape. In the Carpathian mountains, north of Bucharest, the vineyards of **Pietroasele** produce fine sweet wines. **Dobrudja**, bordering the Black Sea, now makes some good varietal wines, from classic varieties introduced by the experimental state research station; Cabernet, Merlot and Pinot Noir have all been successful.

RUSSIA, MOLDAVIA AND UKRAINE

An important sparkling wine industry exists in all three states, mostly made very cheaply by a continuous-flow system. More interesting, however, are the red wines from Moldavia, which include Cabernet and Merlot with the native Saperavi grape, and sweet wines from Crimea.

SLOVAKIA

Slovakia is becoming an important source for inexpensive white varietal wines, particularly Pinot Blanc and Gewürztraminer.

SLOVENIA

The most famous wine from Slovenia is **Lutomer Welschriesling** (which used to be known as Laski Riesling), but the region is capable of producing more interesting wines from Sauvignon, Gewürztraminer and Cabernet-Sauvignon.

CHAPTER NINE

THE WINES OF
THE EASTERN
MEDITERRANEAN

CYPRUS

The Cypriot wine industry used to be based on the production of sherry-style wines, which were banned on Spanish entry to the EC in 1986. It has quickly adapted, however, to making light, fresh, clean wines.

GREECE

Greece is so well known for retsina, white wine to which pine resin is added during fermentation, that it might be assumed that all Greek wines are so made. In fact, about 50 per cent of the wine made in Greece is retsina; the resin was originally added to prevent oxidation, and, having acquired the taste for it, the Greeks continued the practice. Retsina carries a **Traditional Appellation** as it is made throughout Greece.

Greek wines from specified regions have an **Appellation of Origin of Superior Quality**, if they are dry, and **Controlled Appellation of Origin** if they are sweet wines made from Muscat or Mavrodaphne. **Reserve** indicates a minimum ageing period in wood of 2 years for white wines and 3 for red, whilst **Grand Reserve** means 3 years for white and 4 for red. However, it is the name of the producer that is generally a more reliable guide to the quality in the bottle.

The best wines are mostly found in Macedonia – **Naoussa**, **Côtes de Meliton** – and the Peloponnese – **Mavrodaphne** and **Muscat of Patras**, although probably the best Muscat comes from the island of Samos. There are many table wines and Vins de Pays, often made from imported as well as traditional grape varieties, such as the wines from Gentilini in the Ionian islands, which are vinified with modern equipment and show the way forward for other Greek producers, many of whose wines remain dull and oxidized.

ISRAEL

Good-quality wines are now being made from several French varietals in the Golan Heights.

LEBANON

Remarkably, the war-torn Bekaa Valley is home to a fine wine – Château Musar. Produced by Serge Hochar, using Cabernet, Cinsault and Syrah grapes grown on limestone soil at an altitude of 1000 metres, the wine is full-bodied with rich fruit flavours and the capacity to improve with age.

CHAPTER TEN

THE WINES OF
THE NEW WORLD

The term 'New World' is used to describe countries outside the historical birthplace of wine-making around the Mediterranean, principally North and South America, South Africa, Australia and New Zealand. Many of these countries have been growing vines and making wine since colonization by European settlers, but it is really only over the last 30 years that their wines have had a major impact on world markets. Imperial preference in nine-teenth-century Britain gave beneficial duty rates to wines from the Empire, particularly fortified wines from Australia and South Africa, but these were sold on price rather than quality. Today, many of the most exciting and well-made wines are coming from these countries.

AUSTRALIA

Although producing less than 10 per cent of the amount of wine made in either France or Italy, Australia has today stolen a march on nearly every other country in terms of its image, particularly in the United Kingdom. Australian wine is regarded as sound and reliable at the inexpensive end of the market, and innovative and high-quality at the premium level.

Vines were taken to Australia in 1788 by Captain Phillip, the country's first governor. Demand for bulk dry red and cheap fortified wines in the United Kingdom during the latter half of the nineteenth and early twentieth centuries, led to an almost universal production of these types of wine. It has only been in the last 25 years that the Australian wine industry has directed itself to producing lighter styles from premium varietals.

Although wine is produced in every Australian state, the main wine-growing regions are situated in the south-east of the country. The state of South Australia accounts for over 50 per cent of total production, with New South Wales producing just under 30 per cent and Victoria around 13 per cent. There are small but high-quality regions in Tasmania, and particularly south of Perth in Western Australia.

Many Australian wines are blended from grapes grown in different regions and even different states. There is, as yet, no national appellation system; a state-backed scheme exists in Tasmania, and there is a voluntary scheme in Mudgee. Otherwise, there only exists an 'authentication of origin' whereby, if a geographical origin is mentioned, 85 per cent of the wine must be produced there. Many Australian wines have been marketed with European appellation names such as Burgundy and champagne. Agreement was reached in 1994 between Australia and the EC, whereby the former has agreed to phase out the use of these terms and the latter will give protection to Australian names like Coonawarra and

Hunter Valley. It will doubtless be only a matter of time before a national form of protected geographical appellation system is introduced in Australia.

The majority of Australian wines, apart from the inexpensive cask wines (or what we would call a winebox), are sold as varietals – either single or blended. These may carry a very general description of origin, such as South-east Australia, or be more specific, such as Coonawarra. What is equally important, however, is the producer, whose influence on the style of wine will be as, if not more, significant than the source of the grapes.

The most widely planted premium grape varieties in Australia are Shiraz (which is the Australian name for the Syrah of the Rhône Valley) and Cabernet-Sauvignon for red wine and Rhine Riesling, Semillon, Chardonnay and Muscat for white wine. There are also smaller plantings of Pinot Noir, Merlot, Malbec, Grenache and Cinsault among the red varieties, and Sauvignon, Chenin Blanc, Gewürztraminer, Verdelho and Marsanne for white wine.

South Australia

Barossa Valley, Eden Valley and **Adelaide Hills** These three districts make up the oldest and most important region for premium varietal wines, lying to the north-east of Adelaide. White wines, particularly Riesling and Chardonnay, dominate, but excellent Cabernet-Sauvignon and Shiraz are also produced.

Clare/Watervale The most northerly district in South Australia, producing excellent Rhine Riesling and Cabernet-Sauvignon wines.

Coonawarra This district, in the south-eastern corner of the state, is distinguished by its red earth, *terra rossa*, overlying limestone. The water-retentive qualities of the soil, allied to a cooler climate, enable fine Cabernet-Sauvignon, Shiraz and Chardonnay to be made here.

Padthaway/Keppoch North of Coonawarra, produce good Chardonnay, Rhine Riesling and Sauvignon.

McLaren Vale South of Adelaide, produces full-bodied reds from Cabernet and Shiraz.

Riverland A huge quantity of wine is produced in this irrigated area around the Murray river, mostly going into cask wine, but there are some good standard varietals as well.

New South Wales

Hunter Valley North of Sydney, the Lower Hunter Valley vineyards were planted in the last century and produced rich wines from Semillon and Shiraz; the latter was deemed to smell of sweaty saddles. More recently there have been successful plantings in the Upper Hunter Valley, particularly of Chardonnay.

Mudgee To the west of the Hunter Valley is a cooler area producing good Cabernet, Shiraz, Chardonnay and Semillon.

Murrumbidgee Irrigation Area/Riverina   An irrigated area, similar to Riverland on the Murray. Improvements in vinification practices have meant better cask wines and standard quality varietals.

Victoria

Rutherglen   On the Murray river in north-eastern Victoria, this is the home of many of the finest liqueur Muscats (see chapter 7), but good-quality light wines are also now being produced.

Glenrowan/Milawa   Again a classic dessert wine area, but now also producing some fine Cabernet-Sauvignon wines.

Goulburn Valley   This district, north of Melbourne, produces fine white wine from Marsanne, as well as the other varietals.

Yarra Valley   Lying east of Melbourne, this district has one of the coolest climates in Australia. High-quality premium varietals are made from Cabernet, Pinot Noir, Chardonnay and Riesling.

Pyrenees   Produces fine minty red wines and whites from Sauvignon, Riesling and Chardonnay.

Great Western   This district, north-west of Melbourne, is best known for its sparkling wine.

Mildura   Another irrigated district on the Murray river producing cask wines and standard-quality Chardonnay and Sauvignon Blanc.

Tasmania

Very small but high-quality production, particularly in the Pipers Brook area in the north of the island.

Western Australia

Margaret River   200 miles south of Perth, this is currently the most fashionable area in Australia. Mostly made up of small wineries making premium varietals in a climate cooled by its proximity to the Indian Ocean.

Mount Barker/Frankland River   Another cool climate area in the south of the state producing good-quality varietals.

Swan Valley   This district, east of Perth, was traditionally the home of vine-growing in Western Australia, but the very hot climate makes for rather heavy, heady wines.

NEW ZEALAND

New Zealand's wine production is only 10 per cent of that of Australia, but today much of it is of premium quality. This was not always the case; during the 1970s and early 1980s most of New Zealand's vineyards were planted with Müller-Thurgau vines, producing light, slightly sweet white wines in a Germanic style. However, a fall in domestic consumption, allied to lack of interest on export markets for this type of wine, led to the New Zealand Government having to offer large incentives to growers to pull up vines, to counter over-production. Unlike such grants in the EC, there was no ban on growers replanting with other varieties and, since 1985, there has been a dramatic increase in plantings of Sauvignon Blanc and Chardonnay, although Müller-Thurgau still accounts for 25 per cent of total production. It is primarily on its Sauvignons and Chardonnays that the small New Zealand wine industry has achieved enormous acclaim. The United Kingdom accounts for two-thirds of all wines exported.

In addition to Müller-Thurgau, Sauvignon Blanc and Chardonnay, other white varieties planted include Muscat, Riesling, Chenin Blanc, Semillon and Gewürztraminer. Red varieties are led by Cabernet-Sauvignon, with increasing plantings of Pinot Noir, and there is a small amount of Merlot.

The cool maritime climate of New Zealand favours the production of white wines. There is quite a similarity to the climate of Bordeaux throughout New Zealand, but with significantly higher rainfall which can cause serious problems with rot and fungal diseases on the vines.

There is no official system of geographical denomination yet, but the New Zealand Wine Institute has proposed the term Certified Origin.

At the moment, 80 per cent of New Zealand's wine production is in the hands of two firms, both of which have gained recognition for the country's wines. However, it is

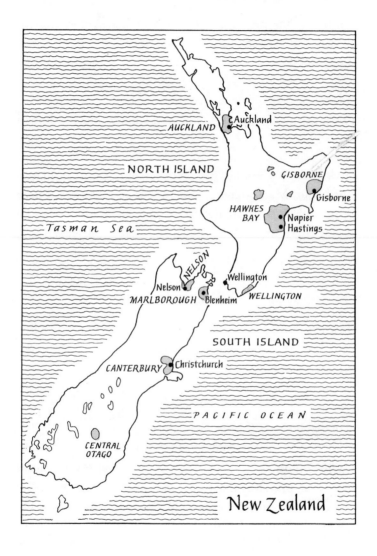

the smaller and medium sized wineries that are now creating
most of the excitement about New Zealand wines.

Wine Regions

The most important areas for grape-growing are:

North Island

Auckland, including the Henderson, Kumeu/Huapai,
Northland, Matakana and Waiheke Island districts: a large
number of wineries are located close to the capital, but a lot
of grapes are trucked in from up to 500 miles away.

Gisborne, including Poverty Bay: traditionally produced
bulk wines from Müller-Thurgau but now making fine
Chardonnay and Gewürztraminer in particular.

Hawke's Bay, on the east coast, produces fine red wines
from Cabernet and Merlot as well as whites from Chardonnay.

Wellington, including Martinborough and Wairarapa districts: small producers of premium-quality wines.

South Island

Marlborough Currently the area undergoing the most
expansion, primarily due to the success of its Pinot Noir and
Chardonnay but most especially Sauvignon Blanc wines.

Nelson An area of small estates producing high-quality

wines benefiting from the highest sunshine levels in the country.

Canterbury   Pinot Noir, Chardonnay and Riesling wines are produced in this cool-climate region around Christchurch.

UNITED STATES OF AMERICA

California

Ninety-five per cent of the wine produced in the USA comes from California. Although vines have been grown in the state since the end of the eighteenth century, it was the 1960s that saw a major expansion of vineyards. Many of these began as relatively small operations, often started by people who had made money elsewhere, and became known as 'boutique wineries'. The number of operating wineries in California trebled between 1965 and 1985.

There are wide variations of climate in the 700-mile length of the state, but it is generally dry in summer, so that irrigation is usually necessary. An important factor on the coastal regions is the fog which rolls in from the Pacific and gives much cooler growing conditions, particularly in the Napa and Sonoma Valleys.

America has its own native species of vines, none of which produce wine remotely of the quality of the European vine, *Vitis vinifera*. It was a Hungarian, Agoston Haraszthy, who was responsible for the introduction of most *vinifera* varieties in the middle of the nineteenth century, including Zinfandel, regarded as California's own grape, but probably the Primitivo from Italy. Premium red wines are also produced from Cabernet-Sauvignon, Merlot and Pinot Noir, and whites from Chardonnay, Sauvignon Blanc (sometimes referred to as Fumé Blanc) and Riesling. Cheap 'jug' wines are usually made from Colombard and Chenin Blanc for whites, Carignan and Barbera for reds.

In 1978 a system of **Approved Viticultural Areas** was introduced, which recognizes the geographical identity of a particular area, but makes no other specific requirement.

Major regions:

North Coast

North of San Francisco, this region includes the three most important districts of Napa Valley, Sonoma County and Mendocino.

Napa Valley runs for 25 miles north of San Francisco Bay. At the southern end, particularly in the Carneros district, the climate is fairly cool with the influence of fog from the Bay, but is much warmer at the northern end around Calistoga. Most of the vineyards are planted on the valley floor. There are more wineries here than in any other district of California and they produce much of the best wine.

Sonoma County, to the west of Napa, was primarily a source of blending wine until the 1960s, since when an

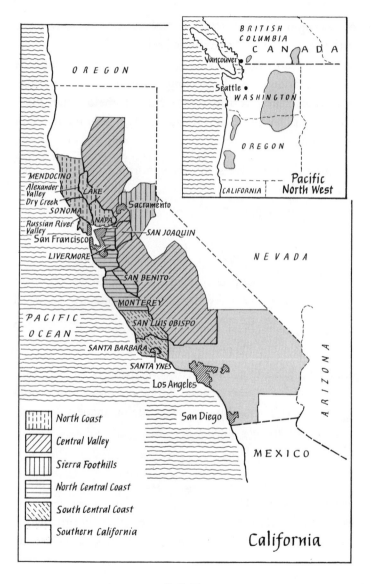

Pacific
North West

North Coast

Central Valley

Sierra Foothills

North Central Coast

South Central Coast

Southern California

California

increasing number of new and existing wineries have made it the second most important district in California. There are significant variations in climate here also, with the southern Sonoma Valley having the coastal fog influence, and warmer areas further north through the Russian River Valley and Dry Creek and Alexander Valley in the north of the county.

Mendocino County is the most northerly of the coastal vineyard districts in California. There has been an increasing amount of new planting of premium varietals in the cooler areas.

North-central Coast

To the south of San Francisco, this has traditionally been an area dominated by a few large firms producing standard wines, but there are also some high-quality small wineries.

South-central Coast

South of Monterey, including the districts of San Luis Obispo, Edna Valley, Santa Barbara County and Santa Ynez Valley. This is by contrast a region made up mostly of premium-quality small wineries.

Central Valley

This lies inland of the coastal regions and has a much warmer climate. The vineyards are planted on the wide valley floor and produce 80 per cent of all Californian wine. This is the home of E. and J. Gallo, the largest wine producer in the world, accounting for one-third of all Californian wine and a production four times greater than that of the whole Champagne region.

Sierra Foothills

Lying between Sacramento and Lake Tahoe. This, the original Gold Rush country of the nineteenth century, has now become a fashionable area for 'boutique' wineries.

The Pacific North-west

The states of Oregon and Washington, are now producing very high-quality wines. With a cooler climate than California, grape varieties like Pinot Noir, Gewürztraminer and Riesling have been especially successful.

New York State

Most wines here are still made from native *labrusca* vines, producing a distinctive 'foxy' flavour, which is often disguised by sweetness, or made into sparkling wine. It was believed that the climate was too harsh for *vinifera* varieties, although there have been some successful plantings over the last 30 years. There are also many hybrid vines, crossings of American *labrusca* and European *vinifera*. The most important area is the Finger Lakes in the north-west of the state.

SOUTH AMERICA

Chile

Chile is only the second largest producer of wine in South America, but undoubtedly makes more of higher quality than its larger neighbour, Argentina. While much of the country's production is bulk wine from the local Pais grape, there are high-quality vineyards in the Central Valley, north and south of the capital, Santiago. Aconagua and the Maipo Valley are the two premier districts, producing fine reds from Cabernet-Sauvignon, Merlot and Malbec, and whites from Sauvignon and Chardonnay. Chile remains unique among major wine-producing countries in that phylloxera has failed to take hold in a country bordered by the Pacific on one side and the Andes on the other.

Argentina

Argentina is the fourth largest wine producer in the world, although much of the production is of modest quality from the Criolla grape (the Pais of Chile). However, in the province of Mendoza, in the west of the country, bordering the Andes, some fine wines are being made, particularly from the red Bordeaux grape varieties – Cabernet-Sauvignon, Merlot and Malbec.

SOUTH AFRICA

The first European settlers planted vines at the Cape of Good Hope in the second half of the seventeenth century. Exports of wine to Great Britain developed during the

French wars of the eighteenth century, and flourished further once the British took over the Cape at the beginning of the nineteenth century. However, the combination, in the latter half of the century, of phylloxera, rapprochement with France and finally the Boer War, caused the collapse of the wine industry. The subsequent slow rebuilding has been given added impetus by the new political freedom in the country, which can only lead to greater things.

The majority of South Africa's vineyards lie in the Southwestern Cape. Although only 35° south of the equator, the climate is tempered by the influence of the Atlantic and Indian Oceans and the cold Benguela current which flows up the west coast of Africa from Antarctica. Good winter rainfall around the Cape Peninsula makes irrigation unnecessary. There are 4 main wine regions:

The Coastal Region, which incorporates the districts of Constantia, Paarl, Stellenbosch, Swartland and Tulbagh, with the Piketberg district to the north.

Breede River Region, which includes the districts of Worcester, Robertson and Swellendam, with the district of Overberg to the south.

Little Karoo Region

Olifants Region

Cinsaut is the most widely planted red varietal in South Africa and is responsible for much of the basic table wine.

Cabernet-Sauvignon is being increasingly planted and is often blended with Cabernet Franc and Merlot; the latter is also sold as a single varietal, giving wines with ripe, plummy fruit. Pinot Noir is producing good wines in the cooler areas. Pinotage, a cross between Pinot Noir and Cinsaut, is unique to South Africa and produces rich, fruity wines.

Chenin Blanc, known as Steen in South Africa, is the most widely planted white variety and produces a wide range of styles, the best usually being fresh, light and crisp. Chardonnay is responsible for some fine wines, both light, clean and dry as well as more complex styles from barrel-fermentation. Fine dry, grassy Sauvignon Blanc and honeyed, flowery Rhine Riesling are also produced.

The Wine of Origin system was introduced in 1973. The Wine and Spirit Board of South Africa issues a certification seal which verifies the origin, vintage and grape variety of the wine.

CHAPTER ELEVEN

BUYING AND STORING WINE

BUYING WINE

Informed advice on wine buying can best be obtained from specialist retailers. Many supermarkets now also provide detailed descriptions of the wines they stock. Wine department managers will also be happy to expand on these. However, the label on the bottle remains every wine buyer's basic guide to the contents, so it is important to be aware of the information the label conveys.

1. The country of origin.
2. The name and address of the bottler (or importer if the wine comes from outside the EC). This will show whether the wine has been bottled by the producer, at the estate, domaine or château, or by a merchant who will have bought, blended and bottled at his cellars the wines of several producers.
3. A batch number if there is more than one bottling of the same wine.
4. The nominal volume, usually 75 cl in a standard bottle.
5. The alcoholic strength, expressed as percentage by volume.
6. If produced within the EC, either the term 'table wine' or a recognized quality designation (such as Appellation Con-

trôlée for French wines) and the specified region (such as Beaujolais).

Each producing country within the EC must register every designated region and implement the necessary requirements in terms of:

a) permitted grape varieties

b) viticultural practices, such as pruning

c) maximum yields

d) wine-making practices, such as the addition of sugar (chaptalization – to increase the alcohol content), or concentrated grape-must (to increase sweetness), or of acid (to increase acidity)

e) alcohol content

f) minimum ageing

g) analysis, and sometimes tasting

If produced outside the EC, either the term 'wine' or a geographical unit (such as Coonawarra).

Any other information is entirely optional. The traditional wine-producing regions of Europe generally provide very little extra detail, with the exception of the vintage (the year the grapes were harvested). There is usually no indication of the grape varieties used, the method of vinification, whether the wine has been aged in casks, and if so for how long, when it was bottled, advice on serving temperature, or the food with which the wine might be enjoyed. Producers from the New World are much more informative on their labels, particularly with the development of varietal wines.

Varietal wines

Consumers of Chablis or Barolo for example, are expected to know that the wines are made from the Chardonnay and Nebbiolo grapes respectively. With the exception of Alsace, the French are proposing to prevent the mention of grape varieties on Appellation Contrôlée wines; all such wines will have to be sold as Vin de Pays.

If a grape variety is mentioned on the label, the wine must be made with at least 85 per cent of that variety (75 per cent in the USA), and if two varieties are listed they must together account for 100 per cent of that wine, with the first-named grape on the label representing the greater proportion.

STORING WINE

Any wines which are going to be kept for longer than a few weeks must be stored correctly. There is no greater disappointment than holding high expectations of a bottle of wine which has been maturing for years, only to find it virtually undrinkable. Today very few houses have traditional underground cellars, and purpose-built ones are extremely expensive. However, it is not too difficult to replicate ideal conditions in some part of most homes. The following are the most important factors to bear in mind.

Temperature

The ideal temperature for storing wine for any length of time is around 12°C. Equally important, though, is to maintain a constant temperature; far better to keep the wine at a steady 10°C or 14°C than to fluctuate between 8°C and 16°C, ending up at an average 12°C, which is what can happen if the wine is stored in a centrally heated room, where the temperature rises and falls during each twenty-four-hour period. As a general rule, wine stored at a higher temperature will mature sooner than if stored at cooler temperature.

Humidity

The ideal humidity for storing wine is 100 per cent; unfortunately this quickly damages the cartons and labels. The best compromise is a relative humidity of around 75–80 per cent at 12°C.

Light

Ultra-violet damages wine, therefore it should always be stored in a dark area.

Smell

Wine can become tainted by smell, through the cork, so a clean atmosphere is important.

Vibration

The maturation of wine can be upset by vibration, so any movement must be avoided if possible.

Storing position

Finally, and most importantly, it must be remembered that all wine bottles must be stored on their sides, if they are to be kept for any length of time. This ensures that the wine keeps the cork moist which would otherwise start to dry and contract and allow air into the bottle. The wine would oxidize very quickly, and become undrinkable.

CHAPTER TWELVE

TASTING AND
SERVING WINE

TASTING WINE

Tasting wine must be viewed as an objective exercise, whereas drinking wine is much more subjective, a question of personal like or dislike. The reason for tasting, rather than just drinking, a wine is to assess its qualities. The taster's aim should be to provide someone who has not tasted a particular wine with as accurate a description as possible. Personal prejudices have to be put aside. Learning to taste is easy; all that is required is a little concentration and an idea of the elements to look for. Tasting wine involves the senses of sight and smell as well as taste.

The appearance of a wine
Clarity

Wine should look clear and bright. If it is cloudy, there is either an intrinsic fault with the wine or it has been badly handled, causing sediment in the bottle to have become mixed with the wine.

Some wines will contain small bubbles of carbon dioxide gas; *pétillance*, as this is known, is encouraged deliberately by some producers, particularly of white wines, to enhance freshness. It is achieved by not allowing all the carbon dioxide produced during fermentation to escape. The best-known example is Muscadet de Sèvre et Maine; if it is labelled 'Sur Lie', it means that the wine has not been racked off the yeast sediment following the alcoholic fermentation, but has been filtered and bottled early, directly from the vat, while some carbon dioxide is still being created.

Sugar-like crystals, often found on the cork or in the bottom of a bottle, are simply tartrates which have been precipitated by cold; they are entirely harmless.

Colour

Colour can give a good indication of the style of wine to be tasted. White wines will vary from pale, watery white to deep, golden yellow, covering all shades in between. The palest-coloured wines usually come from cooler wine-producing regions, such as the Moselle or Loire valleys. Chablis will usually have a pronounced greenish tinge. Many Australian and Californian Chardonnays will be straw-yellow in colour, as a result of the hotter climate in which they are produced. Sweet wines produced from over-ripe, or 'botrytized', grapes will often be a beautiful golden yellow. However, it would be wrong to assume that all sweet wines will be this colour; many sweet German wines, for example, are quite pale. A golden-yellow colour can also be an indication of age; white wines become more yellow as they mature, finally turning brown, which could indicate that they have become oxidized (i.e. they are too old), or, in extreme cases, maderized (i.e. they have taken on the burnt caramel colour of Madeira).

Red wines, when young, will usually be purplish in colour. Light reds, particularly some Italian wines such as Valpolicella and Bardolino, often have a cherry-red colour. Normally, ruby-red is more typical, the deeper-coloured wines again usually indicating warmer climates. As red wines age they take on a more brick-red hue, finally turning tawny and brown. Unlike white wines, these tawny-coloured reds may not be completely oxidized; long ageing in cask prior to bottling is traditional for many Italian wines, and the Pinot Noir grape of Burgundy produces wines which take on an orangey-brown colour much sooner than, for instance, Cabernet-Sauvignon-based wines.

The bouquet or smell of a wine

It is possible to obtain a reasonably good indication of a wine's style from its smell. Any faults not apparent on sight will also be noticeable in the smell. The most common fault, other than an oxidized wine, will be one that is corked. This is the result of a rotten cork, which may have been infected with cork weevil, as a result of a failure in the sterilization process which all wine corks undergo. The wine will smell musty and woody, although there may be no visual indication on the cork itself. A fault which is becoming less and less common, thankfully, is the smell of sulphur, caused by excessive use of sulphur dioxide as an anti-oxidant and anti-yeast agent during the wine-making process.

To gain the most from a wine's bouquet, it is essential to swirl the wine around the glass, which will help release the aromas. Many of the primary elements of the wine – fruit flavours, sweetness, acidity and alcohol – may be noticed. Certain grape varieties have very distinctive aromas – Cabernet-Sauvignon of blackcurrants, Sauvignon Blanc of gooseberries or elderflowers. Sweetness on the nose may not necessarily indicate residual sugar in the wine, as it is not a volatile element. Acidity and alcohol can often be apparent.

Terms describing the bouquet of a wine

Fruity Attractive fruit quality, as in blackcurrants (Cabernet-Sauvignon) or gooseberries (Sauvignon Blanc)

Grapey Often produced by wines with some residual sugar

Floral Flowery aromas such as elderflower (Sauvignon Blanc) or roses (Gewürztraminer)

Grassy Sappy, green smell

Stalky Green, woody (Cabernet Franc)

Vegetal Mature Pinot Noir

Dumb or **closed** Little smell, often from a young or undeveloped wine

Corked See above

Oxidized See above

Acetic Vinegar smell from excess volatile acidity

Sulphury See above

The taste of a wine

Taste should be a confirmation and development of sight and smell. When tasting wine it is important to swirl it well around the mouth. The human tongue picks up sweetness at the tip and acidity at the back. It also helps to draw in air through the teeth to aerate the wine and thereby appreciate its development.

The primary elements of taste

Sweetness Often detected first

Acidity Can carry right through

Alcohol Constitutes part of the body of a wine: a light wine may still be high in alcohol, although a full-bodied wine is rarely low in alcohol

Fruit This can be carried through from the nose but may be more or less intense on the palate

Tannin Tannic acid is found in young red wines, as a result of the skin maceration required to obtain colour. It will leave a dry, slightly bitter taste in the mouth, although the same effect can be the result of wine which has been allowed to age too long, and has lost its fruit and started to dry out.

A wine in which all these elements are in balance will appear complete, although it must be remembered that a young red wine may have noticeably high levels of tannin until it reaches maturity.

Terms describing the taste of a wine

SWEETNESS

Dry   Wine with all its grape sugars fermented out
Sweet   Wine containing residual grape sugars

ACIDITY

Fresh, crisp, green, sharp, tart Noticeable or excessive acidity
Flat, flabby Lack of acidity

ALCOHOL

Body   A light, medium or full-bodied wine is determined by the amount of alcohol and extract
Extract   The soluble solids in a wine
Thin   Wine with little extract or body
Big   Wine with plenty of extract and alcohol
Heavy   Wine with too much extract and alcohol

FRUIT

Ripe   Wine made from mature grapes
Rich   Wine full of fruit, alcohol and extract
Nutty   Often the taste of full, dry white wines
Spicy   Often found in wines from the Syrah grape
Peppery   Often found in wines from the Grenache grape
Neutral   Bland, little fruit flavour
Oxidized   Flat, stale, lacking fruit flavour
Mouldy, musty, woody   'Off' flavours – perhaps corked wine

TANNIN

Hard, tough   Excess of tannin
Round, smooth, soft, supple   Little tannin

Finally, it is important to appreciate the length of time the taste remains after swallowing or spitting out the wine. This is known as the after-taste or finish and its length is a good indicator of quality – a wine can be described as having good length. When little taste remains after swallowing, a wine is described as short.

SERVING WINE

The enjoyment of wine is greatly enhanced if it is served correctly. This requires a little forethought, particularly as far as serving temperature is concerned.

Temperature

White and rosé wines are best served around 7°C. The best way to chill wine is to put the bottle into a refrigerator for a couple of hours. If the wine is going to be drunk sooner, then 15 minutes in a bucket of ice and water, or in a freezer, will achieve the same result. However, it is important to remember that too cold a temperature will deaden the bouquet and flavour of a wine.

Sparkling wines should be served well chilled, 5–7°C; the

low temperature helps to reduce the pressure of carbon dioxide gas in the bottle.

Light fortified wines, such as pale dry, fino or manzanilla sherry should also be served well chilled. It is also not uncommon to serve light tawny port chilled; otherwise, fortified wines are best served at ambient room temperature.

Red wines are traditionally served at what is called 'room' temperature. This term originated before central heating, and nowadays there is a tendency to serve red wine too warm. But there is also a fashion for serving some light red wines, particularly those from the Loire Valley, chilled. Certainly, lighter styles such as these, or Beaujolais, or Valpolicella and Bardolino from Italy, are often best served cool, around 12°C. Fuller-bodied red wines are best served warmer, around 16°C. It is dangerous to try to raise a red wine's temperature quickly; if the wine is 'cooked' or 'boiled' it will be completely spoilt. If a red wine cannot be allowed to rise to ambient room temperature naturally and slowly, it can be put in a bucket of warm, not hot water, but it should never be put under boiling water, in an oven or on a radiator.

Opening

Many red wines benefit from being opened some time before serving. As a general rule, the younger and more full-bodied the wine, the longer it will need to breathe. Old wines should only be opened up to an hour before drinking, as they can deteriorate very quickly once they have come in contact with air. Otherwise a couple of hours is generally sufficient.

Corkscrews

The best corkscrews for opening bottles of wine will have a broad wire spiral which ensures good purchase on the cork, whereas a thick screw can pull out a hole through the middle of a cork.

Decanting

Red wines which have been made to mature in the bottle will begin to throw a sediment after a number of years. It is therefore always safer to decant a wine more than 10 years old, in order to separate the wine from the deposit in the bottle. Decanting also helps to aerate a wine as it is being poured, and so also serves to soften full-bodied, young red wines.

Glasses

The enjoyment of any wine is enhanced by serving it in good glasses. The best glasses for wine are the simplest, made of clear, thin glass, narrower at the lip than in the bowl to concentrate the bouquet, and with a stem long enough to keep the hand away from the bowl. Glasses, especially for red wine, should be generous in size; they should be no more than two-thirds filled to allow space for the bouquet to develop as the wine is swirled around the glass. Finally, it is important to ensure that glasses are clean and not carrying any smell of detergent.

Keeping opened wine

Once a wine has been opened the exposure to the air means that it will start to oxidize and deteriorate. The length of time any opened wine can be kept depends not only on the wine itself, but also on the amount left in the bottle in proportion to the air. A bottle with only one glassful taken from it will last for 3 or 4 days, whereas a bottle with one glassful remaining in it may not be drinkable the following day. White wines which have been opened should always be kept in the refrigerator, and red wines keep better in a cool place. Wines made from certain grape varieties, notably Pinot Noir and Gamay, do not really keep at all well, whereas others, such as Nebbiolo, can actually improve the day after being opened.

Various products claim to maintain freshness in an opened bottle of wine; the best system is an inert gas spray which, being heavier than air, forms a blanket on top of the wine.

WINE AND FOOD

Most wines taste different when tasted on their own or drunk with food. Different elements in each react with each other. Traditionally, matching wine and food had little to do with anything other than geographical association. For centuries, the purpose of wine production was simply to provide wine for meals. While different areas discovered that certain grape varieties and styles were better suited to their climate and soil than others, wines were primarily being made to suit the local foods.

The increasing consumption of wine without food has contributed to the popularity of New World wines with their ripe, sweet fruit flavours and soft tannins. A lot of these wines have a variety of flavours which often conflict with the different flavours in many dishes; they are at their best accompanying simple roast or grilled foods. Many Italian red wines, on the other hand, can taste rather dry and astringent on their own, but soften dramatically when drunk with food, especially a cuisine based on olive oil. German wines, generally light in body and slightly sweet are best drunk on their own.

There are two specific criteria for matching wine with food. First, the two must complement each other: a strong-tasting food will kill a light wine, just as a rich, full-bodied wine will overwhelm light food. Muscadet and Chablis are perfect with shellfish but would be killed by game. Equally important is contrast. A wine with good acidity and dryness can be a perfect match for oily food – Sancerre, or New Zealand Sauvignon Blanc, with smoked salmon, for example – while claret, with its dry tannins, is the perfect complement to the fattiness of lamb.

Certain combinations which have developed over the

years can seem strange. The most striking is drinking Sauternes with *foie gras*; one of the richest foods accompanied by rich, strong, sweet white wine. An equally good match would be a strong, dry, spicy white from Alsace.

When selecting wine to match a specific dish, it is important to remember that it is not just a question of choosing the wine to match the particular type of meat or fish; the sauce in which they are cooked can have greater effect on the wine. Cream- or butter-based sauces demand wines with acidity rather than alcohol to help cut the richness; Sauvignon grape-based wines, Bourgogne Aligote or Muscadet for white wines; cool-climate red wines, such as those from the Loire Valley, Beaujolais, or even light Burgundy. Dishes rich in oil need dry, full-bodied wines, such as whites or roses from southern France, or Bordeaux or Piedmontese red wines. Hot, spicy foods will kill just about any wine, and are best accompanied by water or beer.

One of the hardest ingredients with which to match wine is vinegar, its natural antithesis. Any dish with a dressing containing vinegar will be detrimental to wine. The best solution for salad dishes is to serve a full-bodied, dry white wine with low acidity. Chocolate is also difficult, but not impossible – a fortified Muscat, such as Beaumes de Venise with its orangey sweetness, can make a good match, as can rich Australian Liqueur Muscat, or Malaga from Spain.

Strong, dry cheeses are usually best eaten with red wine, but this is not the ideal accompaniment to all cheese. Creamy blue cheeses can often be delicious with sweet white wine. Port may be fine for Stilton, but only if it is drunk with it, not poured into it.

If you are serving several different wines during a meal, and especially if they are its focal point, it is important to serve them in the right order:

Dry before sweet
Light before full-bodied
Young before old

FOOD	STYLE OF WINE	SUGGESTION
FISH DISHES		
Terrine	Light dry white	Chablis
Soups		Sancerre/Pouilly
Mayonnaise	Crisp dry white	Fumé
Buttery sauce		Burgundy
Smoked		
Chinese-style	Spicy white	Alsace
Barbecued		Tokay/Riesling
CHICKEN DISHES		
Mayonnaise	Clean, dry white	Soave
Buttery sauce		
Chinese-style	Full white	Mâcon
Roast	Light, fruity red	Beaujolais
Casseroled		
Barbecued/Indian/ Tandbori	Fuller red	Côtes du Rhône
VEAL		
Buttery sauce	Light, fruity red	Valpolicella
Roast		
Casserole	Fuller red	Chianti Classico

PORK

Buttery sauce	Light red	Beaujolais
Spicy/Chinese style		Villages
Stewed/Cassoulet	Full red	Corbières
Roast	Medium red	Burgundy
Barbecued		

LAMB

With Hollandaise	Light to medium red	Chinon/Bourgueil
Stewed	Fuller red	Claret/Rioja
Roast		
Spiced/curried/ barbecued	Spicy red	Crozes-Hermitage

BEEF

With Hollandaise	Medium red	Burgundy
Casserole	Fuller red	Rhone/Châteauneuf du Pape
Roast		
Spiced/barbecued	Full, spicy red	Australian Shiraz Australian/ Californian Cabernet

VENISON	Rich red	Australian Shiraz
DUCK	Medium red	Burgundy
GAME BIRDS	Full red	Claret
COLD COLLATIONS/ SALAMIS	Rosé or light red	Tavel Rosé Valpolicella
PÂTÉS/TERRINES	Spicy red	Côtes du Rhône

FOIS GRAS	Sweet white	Sauternes
SOUPS		
Light	Fortified	Dry sherry/Madeira
Creamy	Dry white	Burgundy
VEGETABLE DISHES	Light dry white	Soave
CHEESE		
Soufflé		Alsace Tokay
Soft, creamy	Light, sweet white	Loire (Coteaux du Layon)
Blue		
Hard	Medium red	Burgundy
PUDDINGS		
Plain fruit	Slightly sweet white	German Spätlese/Auslese
Light fruit puddings	Sweet white	Coteaux du Layon
Ice creams/sorbets		Italian Moscato
Rich creamy puddings	Rich, sweet, white	Sauternes
		Champagne
Hot soufflés	Sweet	
Chocolate puddings	Fortified	Muscat de Beaumes de Venise
		Australian Liqueur Muscat

WINE STYLE	*STYLE OF FOOD*
Very dry white (Muscadet, Sauvignon grape wines, Chablis)	Shellfish, salmon, oily fish
Dry white (Soave, Frascati, Chardonnay wines, Burgundy)	White fish

229

Spicy dry white (Alsace, some dry German and English wines)	Smoked fish
Medium dry white (Moselle, Vouvray, Vinho Verde)	Chicken
Medium sweet white (German Spätlese/Auslese, Italian Moscato)	Soft, creamy cheese Fruit and fruit puddings
Sweet white (Sauternes, Barsac, Muscat de Beaumes de Venise)	Foie gras Rich puddings Chocolate puddings
Rosé (Tavel, Provence)	Bouillabaisse Cold meats
Light red (Beaujolais, Valpolicella)	Chicken, Veal Pork
Soft red (Burgundy)	Pork, Duck
Medium red (Claret, Côtes du Rhône, Chianti, Rioja)	Lamb, Game birds
Full red (Châteauneuf du Pape, Cabernet-Sauvignon wines)	Beef
Very full red (Croyes-Hermitage, Barolo, Australian Shiraz)	Rich stews, Venison

ACKNOWLEDGEMENTS

This book would never have been written without the encouragement and help of all the staff at Leith's School, particularly Caroline Waldegrave. Special thanks are due to Richard Mayson, who wrote the chapters on Iberia and fortified wines, Eleanor Smith, who checked and corrected the manuscript, Neil Hyslop, who drew the maps, Bill Sanderson for the drawings, Helen Dore the copyeditor and Charlie Hartley at Bloomsbury.

INDEX

INDEX